WITHDRAWN

CULTURES OF THE WORLD
Uganda

Cavendish Square
New York

Published in 2019 by Cavendish Square Publishing, LLC
243 5th Avenue, Suite 136, New York, NY 10016

Library of Congress Cataloging-in-Publication Data

Names: Barlas, Robert, author. | Yong, Jui Lin, author. | Griffin, Brett, author.
Title: Uganda / Robert Barlas, Yong Jui Lin, and Brett Griffin.
Description: [Third edition] | New York : Cavendish Square, 2019. |
Series: Cultures of the world | Includes bibliographical references and index. |
Audience: Grade 6+.
Identifiers: LCCN 2018054995 (print) | LCCN 2018056023 (ebook) |
ISBN 9781502647412 (ebook) | ISBN 9781502647405 (library bound)
Subjects: LCSH: Uganda--Juvenile literature.
Classification: LCC DT433.22 (ebook) | LCC DT433.22 .B37 2019 (print) |
DDC 967.61--dc23
LC record available at https://lccn.loc.gov/2018054995

Editorial Director: David McNamara
Editor: Kristen Susienka
Copy Editor: Nathan Heidelberger
Associate Art Director: Alan Sliwinski
Designer: Jessica Nevins
Production Coordinator: Karol Szymczuk
Photo Research: J8 Media

CONTENTS

UGANDA TODAY

ON THE NORTHERN SHORE OF LAKE VICTORIA LIES THE COUNTRY of Uganda. Once claimed as a protectorate by the British Empire, the East African nation was created through the combination of different tribes and ethnic groups into one territory bordered by lakes and mountains. Long exploited as a British colonial possession, Uganda gained its independence in 1962. The legacy of the colonial period has lingered beyond the granting of official sovereignty, however, and echoes of it are still heard today.

RESTORING ORDER

The last fifty years have seen the country experience military dictatorship, civil war, and domestic insurrection as it has struggled to adjust to independence. While a stable government was finally put in place in the late 1980s, it has not meant an end to the challenges facing Uganda.

In the twentieth and twenty-first centuries, under President Yoweri Museveni, who took power in 1986, the government has made significant advances in restoring a measure of basic order to the country. The economy has been brought back from a state of collapse in the 1980s, and much of the nation's infrastructure, damaged during the periods of dictatorship and civil war, has been rebuilt. A constitution was drafted in 1995, and regular elections have taken place at five-year intervals ever since. This young democracy is under threat now, however, as President Museveni has become increasingly reluctant to relinquish power. The constitution has been altered to scrap any limitations on the length of his presidency, and opposing politicians are being targeted by the state's security forces. Voices in the press that question the administration have been suppressed, and freedom of expression has been stifled in important ways. As Uganda looks to be slipping back toward autocracy, its people are more determined than ever to defend their democracy.

UGANDANS TODAY

Over forty million people live in Uganda. They are a diverse bunch, coming from a variety of ethnic and tribal backgrounds and speaking more than thirty languages. Whether urban or rural in origin, Ugandans are united by the struggles of their daily lives. One-third of the population lives in poverty, and many people rely on a precarious source of income that could disappear at any time. The majority of Uganda's labor force works in the agricultural sector, and a single bad harvest can have devastating effects on their ability to meet their needs. To make matters worse, inconsistent rainfall and droughts have been increasing as a result of climate change, contributing to a rise in poverty and food shortages in certain regions of the country. Climate change has also increased sudden downpours, causing floods that wash away homes and fields and leave pools of contaminated water behind.

The Ugandan health-care sector is ill prepared to meet many disease outbreaks, particularly in the wake of the HIV/AIDS epidemic that has ravaged Uganda over the last few decades. The populations most vulnerable to HIV are women and the LGBT community, both of which already face discrimination in their daily lives. Gender roles in Uganda are rigidly enforced, with much of the country still subscribing to traditional tribal notions of masculinity and femininity. When combined with the revival of fundamentalist, right-wing

Christianity in the last decade, these attitudes also lead to extreme persecution of the country's gay community, and homosexuality remains against Ugandan law. Women are on average poorer and less educated than men, and they are experiencing increasing rates of domestic abuse and sexual assault. All of these struggles start at a young age, as the majority of children in Uganda fail to complete secondary school, dropping out to work or to help their parents on their farms.

The youth of Uganda are poised to make major strides in addressing their country's political and social injustices in the years to come.

THE ROAD AHEAD

In the face of these hardships, Ugandans remain defiant. The cities play host to a bustling nightlife, while traditional festivals and ceremonies continue to color life in rural communities. Burgeoning communities of artists have grown up across the country, from filmmakers in the slums of Kampala to musicians in the halls of Parliament, challenging the power of the government and giving expression to the pain felt by so many of their fellow citizens. A new generation of Ugandans is also poised to make its voice heard, pushing back against the everyday inequalities it faces. Protests against the entrenched power of the government persist in the face of police oppression, and activists have been beaten and arrested standing up for the rights of women and the LGBT community. Grassroots initiatives to combat climate change have been implemented on a national scale by the country's Parliament, and thousands of acres of protected wilderness have been created. International organizations have partnered with local institutions to deliver much-needed health care to underserved communities and to combat food insecurity. Across all sectors of society, the Ugandan people are looking after one another and attempting to assert control over their own lives. It is not yet clear what the effects of these attempts will be, but it is only through such collective action that progress will be made in addressing the many inequities that characterize life in Uganda today.

GEOGRAPHY

The Ugandan kob, a species of antelope, is one of many animals native to the savannas of Uganda.

LOCATED IN EASTERN AFRICA, Uganda is a landlocked country with a tropical climate. Its landscape is mostly plateau surrounded by mountains, though lakes and swampland account for about 20 percent of the surface area. The climate supports a vast array of flora and fauna across several ecosystems, including savanna and both tropical and subtropical forest. Uganda shares its borders with South Sudan in the north, Kenya in the east, Tanzania and Rwanda in the south, and the Democratic Republic of the Congo (DRC) in the west.

Uganda is 93,065 square miles (241,038 square kilometers) in size. This makes it slightly smaller than the US state of Oregon.

CLIMATE PATTERNS

Overall, Uganda has what is called a modified tropical climate, which is mainly mild and pleasant. There are usually around twelve hours of sunlight a day, and temperatures remain steady throughout the year. Within the country, however, climate patterns vary between regions, most notably in respect to temperature and rainfall. At the higher elevations in the west, mean annual temperatures are approximately

The highest point in Uganda is Margherita Peak on Mount Stanley in the Rwenzori Mountains. It rises 16,765 feet (5,110 m) above sea level and is the third-highest peak in Africa. The first person to climb it was Luigi Amedeo Abruzzi. He led an expedition there in 1906. He named the peak "Margherita," in honor of the queen of Italy at the time.

ten degrees lower than in the lowlands of the northeast. Rainfall also varies from region to region. Uganda has two rainy seasons, from March to May and from September to November. The highest levels of rainfall occur around Lake Victoria in the south of the country. By contrast, the northeastern regions are semiarid and are home to dry savanna. As a result of climate change, prolonged droughts, massive flooding, and hailstorms are occurring across Uganda with increasing frequency, disrupting agricultural production and leading to a rise in infectious diseases.

MOUNTAINS AND LAKES

While much of Uganda is a plateau, marked by numerous small hills, valleys, and savannas, the entire country lies in a cradle of mountains. The volcanic Virunga Mountains lie in the southwest, along the borders between Uganda, Rwanda, and the DRC. The Rwenzori Mountains are in the west, crossing the border into the DRC north of Lake Edward. In the center of the range, six peaks have permanent snow or glaciers. As a result of climate change, however, much of the glacial coverage in the Rwenzori Mountains has receded.

On the border with Kenya in the east towers Mount Elgon, an extinct volcano and once the highest mountain in Africa. Over the years, erosion and other geological forces have reduced its peak to its present height, 14,177 feet

(4,321 meters). On the wooded slopes, great caves, gorges, and waterfalls present some of the most exciting scenery in Uganda, and the terraced coffee plantations and bamboo forests enhance the wonderful views.

In addition to its rim of mountains, Uganda is also characterized by its lakes. The largest of these is the famous Lake Victoria, which Uganda shares with Kenya and Tanzania. This is the largest lake in Africa and the second-largest body of freshwater in the world. Uganda's western border runs through the Western Rift Valley, which is dotted from north to south by lakes, including Lake Albert, Lake Edward, and Lake George. The lakes provide various attractions, including swimming, sailing, and excellent fishing—Nile perch in Lake Victoria can weigh as much as 220 pounds (100 kilograms)!

Mount Elgon is home to a wide variety of unique plant life.

FLORA AND FAUNA

Most of Uganda is lush and fertile, with the country's varied climates giving rise to a diverse array of plant life. Much of the country's vegetation is in the flat savannas of the east and northeast, while in the areas of high rainfall there are many trees typical of the rain forest. There is also a small area of semidesert in the north and the northeast, where drought-resistant bushes, grasses, and succulent plants grow. Evergreen trees cover a large part of the country, and there are rolling hills and meadows in the west. Much of southern Uganda was formerly covered by forests, but most of these have been cleared for human settlement.

Uganda is also home to a wide variety of animal life, including hundreds of species of mammals and over one thousand different kinds of birds. The biggest Ugandan land animals are the elephant, the rhinoceros, and the giraffe, most of which live in the country's national parks. Several big cats, including lions, leopards, and cheetahs, can also be seen in the savannas of Uganda's animal preserves. The Bwindi Impenetrable National Park, located in the southwest,

The Nile River, the longest river in the world, has its source in Uganda. It originates in Lake Victoria and takes on different names as it flows through the country. From Lake Victoria it flows north to Lake Kyoga and Lake Albert as the Victoria Nile. There, it joins the waters of the Albert Nile and enters South Sudan, where it is called the White Nile. White-water rapids and numerous waterfalls, such as the spectacular Murchison Falls, mark the Nile's course. Along most of its length, the banks are thick with a variety of plant life and water birds, and the more tranquil stretches provide watering spots for the multitude of game that inhabit its shores. Giant Nile crocodiles are seen at many points along the river, either basking in the sun or floating stealthily on the surface of the water.

The Nile crocodile is one of the deadliest predators found in Uganda.

is home to half the world's remaining population of mountain gorillas. Other primates found in Uganda include chimpanzees, baboons, and the black-and-white Abyssinian colobus. In the country's many rivers and lakes can be found hippopotamuses and crocodiles. One of the continent's most dangerous predators, crocodiles can grow to more than 16 feet (5 m) long. Although they are primarily fish eaters, they are responsible for more human deaths than any other vertebrate in Africa. Other reptiles include the rock python, one of the largest snakes in the world, and the venomous and aggressive black mamba.

NATIONAL PARKS

Numerous national parks and game reserves provide a showcase for Uganda's wild animals and spectacular scenery. The parks display the extraordinary landscapes and natural features of the country—freshwater lakes, swamps, mountains, forests, woodlands, rolling plains, and grasslands. To protect and effectively manage these invaluable resources on a sustainable basis, the Uganda National Parks Department was established in 1952. In 1996, the Uganda Wildlife Authority, a semi-autonomous agency, assumed responsibility for managing the country's national parks and wildlife reserves. Today, they oversee ten national parks and twelve wildlife reserves, as well as thirteen wildlife sanctuaries and other areas. In total, the parks and reserves occupy over 4,292 square miles (11,116 square kilometers).

Uganda's national parks are home to more than half the world's remaining population of mountain gorillas.

In addition to the Bwindi Impenetrable National Park, which encompasses 124 square miles (321 sq km) in the southwest of the country, the 13-square-mile (33 sq km) Mgahinga Gorilla National Park provides a unique opportunity to see some of the world's largest mountain gorillas—although it requires a lengthy hike to track them down. Mount Elgon National Park is in the southeast of the country and surrounds Mount Elgon. Mount Elgon is one of the best places to see the many varieties of Ugandan birds.

In the Kibale National Park, chimpanzees, monkeys, and beautiful forest birds are common. One of Uganda's most significant national parks, the Rwenzori Mountains National Park, provides some of the best (and most difficult) hiking opportunities in the country. Nearby is the Semuliki National Park, an eastern extension of the vast Ituri Forest, which is small but offers visitors two important attractions: refreshing hot springs and more than four hundred species of birds.

In the northwest lies Murchison Falls National Park, Uganda's largest national park, with its spectacular waterfalls on the Nile River. Along with Queen Elizabeth National Park and Lake Mburo National Park in the southwest, as well as the remote Kidepo Valley National Park in the northeast, Murchison Falls National Park provides some of the country's best opportunities to see big-game animals in the country. These parks are all flat savannas with plenty of wide-open spaces in which the animals roam freely.

URBAN CENTERS

Around 24 percent of the Ugandan population lives in cities. The largest city in Uganda is the capital, Kampala, which has a population of approximately

The crested crane is Uganda's national emblem and is depicted on Uganda's flag. It lives along lakes, swamps, and grasslands, where it can be found in large flocks. The bird's plumage is mostly gray but also includes splashes of red, yellow, and black, the colors of Uganda's flag. The crane adorning the flag has one leg raised, symbolizing that Uganda is moving forward into the future and not standing still. Uganda's crested cranes can most commonly be seen in Murchison Falls National Park.

2.9 million people. Other major cities include Mbarara, Gulu, Entebbe, Jinja, and Masaka. Uganda's cities typically contain large numbers of young people, and more men than women. Migration to cities from rural areas has been an ongoing result of the poverty experienced by many Ugandans, who are able to make a better living working manual labor or service jobs in the cities than on farms.

JINJA An important commercial center in Uganda is the city of Jinja. It is situated on the banks of Lake Victoria at the source of the Nile, 50 miles (80 km) east of Kampala. Jinja is the home of the Nalubaale Hydroelectric Power Station (formerly Owen Falls Dam), which supplies power to most of Uganda as well as to parts of Kenya and Rwanda.

KAMPALA Located on the northern shores of Lake Victoria at an altitude of 3,900 feet (1,190 m), Kampala is the heart of Uganda. It is both the center of commercial life and the seat of government. The city is spread out over several hills, including Mengo Hill, where the kabaka (ka-BA-ka), or king, of Buganda had his court. In 1890, the British established a settlement there. The town grew to municipal status in 1949, and it became the capital city of the newly independent Uganda in 1962. The climate of Kampala is typical of an inland tropical city. Temperatures range from a high of 81 degrees Fahrenheit (27 degrees Celsius) to a low of 63°F (17°C), depending on the season.

Kampala is a mix of modern construction and extreme poverty. Within the center of the city are gardens and parks, as well as many important government, educational, and cultural institutions. The Parliament Building is in Kampala, as is Makerere University and the National Theater. The Botanical Gardens, founded in 1898, were originally natural forest used as a research center for the introduction of exotic fruits and plants to Uganda. Many of these fruits can be bought fresh in Kampala's Nakasero Market. In and around the city, however, are extensive slums. Tens of thousands of Ugandans live in dire poverty in these areas, usually in crude dwellings built from wood, earth, and scrap materials. These Ugandans have little to no access to the electricity or sanitation enjoyed by their wealthier neighbors.

Crude shacks and modern construction exist within blocks of one another in Kampala, the capital city of Uganda.

INTERNET LINKS

http://ugandawildlife.org
The homepage of the Uganda Wildlife Authority, this site provides information about the history of the organization as well as detailed descriptions of all of the country's national parks.

https://www.worldatlas.com/webimage/countrys/africa/ug.htm
The World Atlas includes maps of Uganda as well as information about the country's geography, history, and important figures.

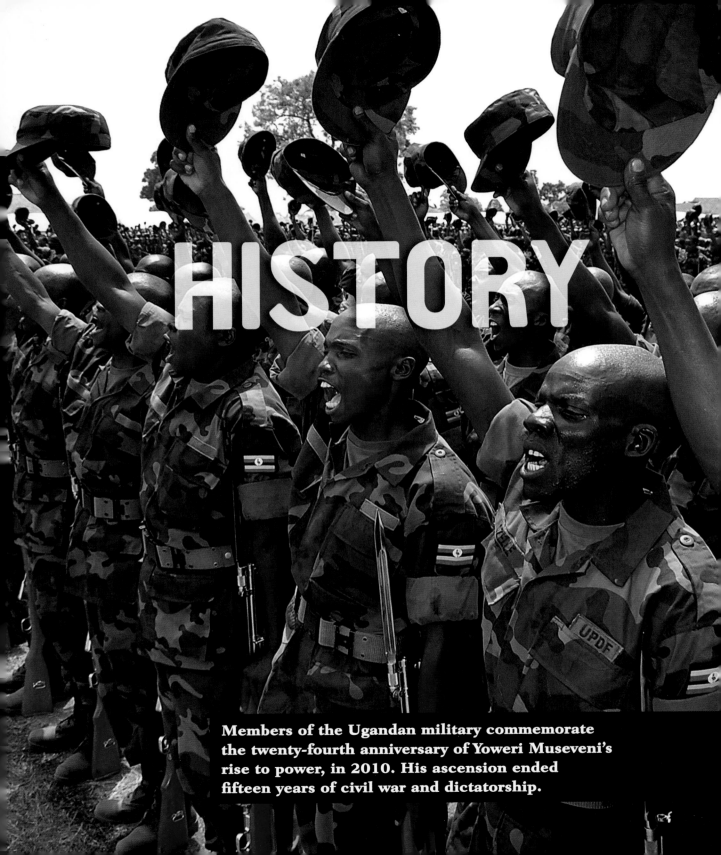

HISTORY

Members of the Ugandan military commemorate
the twenty-fourth anniversary of Yoweri Museveni's
rise to power, in 2010. His ascension ended
fifteen years of civil war and dictatorship.

2

THE HISTORY OF UGANDA, LIKE THE history of most of its African neighbors, is marked by European imperialism and the challenges that have followed upon gaining independence.

Once a region ruled over by local tribal chieftains, the modern nation of Uganda was formed by the British Empire, which combined several unrelated tribes into an area with arbitrarily drawn borders. Though Uganda was never formally colonized, its resources were extracted for the benefit of the British Empire, and the degree of autonomy allowed its people was in direct relation to their willingness to agree to British rule.

In 1962, after a growing independence movement, Uganda was finally granted political sovereignty, but problems remained. The country was still very poor and dependent on Western powers, and was also divided along ethnic lines. This led to a military coup in 1971, followed by a decade of dictatorship that caused the deaths of hundreds of thousands of Ugandans. After several further political upheavals and a civil war, Yoweri Museveni came to power in 1986, and he has remained president ever since. Under Museveni, Uganda has finally been able to maintain a stable political system, but it is one that has become increasingly undemocratic. Museveni has also managed to cultivate good relations with both Western nations and, more recently, China, but these relationships have been neocolonial in nature, with European and Chinese corporations making vast profits off of investments in the country that provide little value to the average Ugandan. Though it has been more than fifty years since independence, the legacy of imperialism continues to shape Uganda today.

The borders of modern-day Uganda were drawn by the British during the late nineteenth century.

THE KINGDOM OF BUGANDA AND ITS NEIGHBORS

Though written records of Uganda's past date back only as far as the mid-nineteenth century, the region was inhabited from a very early date. The Bantu peoples were engaged in agriculture in what is now Uganda from as early as 1000 BCE, and ironworking has been traced back to 1000 CE. During the seventeenth and eighteenth centuries, powerful social and political orders developed among the Bantu peoples, including the Bunyoro, Buganda, Busoga, Ankole, and Toro kingdoms, which made profitable links with the Sudanese slave trade that underpinned the regional economy. By the nineteenth century, the kingdom of Buganda, the largest in the region, was allied to the powerful Shirazi of Zanzibar and gained influence and control over its smaller, less powerful neighbors. The Buganda kingdom was made up of people of the Baganda ethnic group.

Although there were many tribes and people of different ethnic origins in the area that is now Uganda, for many years the kingdom of Buganda represented the real power in the land, and the kabaka, or king, was the supreme authority, with power over the life and death of his subjects. The kabaka was aided by a lukiko (LOO-chee-ko), a council of trusted advisers that could occasionally act as a check to his power. Buganda's relations with its neighbors and subjects could be benign and even beneficial, but could also be exploitative, as smaller kingdoms were taken advantage of to secure the kabaka's power.

THE BRITISH IN UGANDA

From its rise to power in the 1600s until the 1860s, Buganda and its kings enjoyed a time of relatively untroubled power, with little interference from outside forces. That situation changed permanently with the arrival of the

Before the British arrived in Buganda, the kingdom's interactions with the world outside its immediate region occurred through Muslim and Arab traders, who began arriving in the 1830s and 1840s. Among other things, they brought Islam to the kingdom, and Uganda continues to have a minority Muslim population to this day. As for the British public, their first exposure to Buganda and its king came in the form of stories told by explorers (including the legendary Henry Morton Stanley, who met Mutesa I in 1875), as well as a letter purportedly written by the kabaka to Queen Victoria stating that he wished to be a "friend to the white people."

British in the late 1800s. The first British citizens to enter Buganda were explorers looking for the source of the Nile River in 1862 (among them was John Speke, who named Lake Victoria for the English monarch at the time, Queen Victoria). The explorers were soon followed by Christian missionaries, both Protestant and Catholic, who were welcomed into the region by the ruling kabaka, Mutesa I. The kabaka hoped that the missionaries might be able to help him with military matters, including providing advanced European weaponry. He was also wary of pushing back too strongly against the Europeans, whose superior military capabilities could threaten his rule more effectively than any other local kingdom. During his reign, Mutesa I welcomed European trade and allowed both Catholic and Protestant missionaries (as well as Muslim traders) to believe that he agreed with their particular religious teachings. The close proportion of Catholics (39 percent) and Protestants (45 percent) in Uganda today is the result of Mutesa I's shrewd decision not to show any one denomination preference.

Mutesa I died in 1884, and he was succeeded by his son, Mwanga II. Less welcoming of foreign interference than his father, Mwanga II attempted to expel the missionaries that had taken up residence in Buganda. This led to his deposition as kabaka and sent a clear signal to the British that they needed to assume more formal control of the region. Though Mwanga II was eventually allowed to retake the throne, it was with the clear understanding that the British were now in charge. A series of treaties drawn up in the late

This 1864 woodcut depicts the kabaka of Buganda reviewing his troops in the years before the British assumed full control over the region.

1880s and early 1890s allowed the Imperial British East Africa Company to establish itself in Buganda, and in 1894 the kingdom was declared a British protectorate. In the following years, the neighboring regions to the north were added to the protectorate, establishing the modern-day borders of Uganda. This forced combination of disparate peoples (the centralized Bantu kingdoms of the south together with the decentralized Nilotic and Sudanic peoples of the north) would make it much harder for residents of Uganda to forge a shared national identity upon independence, a major factor in the struggles faced in the 1960s and 1970s.

Mwanga II reluctantly went along with these treaties, but he eventually attempted to lead a revolt in 1897. It was swiftly suppressed by the British, and he was exiled permanently from the country. His infant son was made kabaka in his stead, and the British assumed de facto control of the region. The Buganda Agreement of 1900 formalized the new order. The kabaka was recognized as the nominal ruler of Buganda so long as he remained faithful to the British; his council of chiefs would also receive recognition and parcels of land, as long as they, too, agreed to support the British in their endeavors. Similar arrangements were drawn up with other kingdoms in the protectorate, and the region was brought firmly under the control of the British Foreign Office by 1905. The hundreds of years of Buganda rule had come to an end.

MOVING INTO THE TWENTIETH CENTURY

During the first half of the twentieth century, the British treated Uganda like the rest of its imperial holdings, i.e., as a means of generating wealth. Coffee and cotton production were quickly institutionalized across the protectorate, and sugar production soon followed. Railways were built to improve communications and speed up the transport of goods. Schools were also established by the British, in an effort to produce a class of men well-versed in British traditions of government and law, thereby creating a group of native Africans more amenable to British rule. These efforts were primarily focused

Uganda's status as a protectorate meant that it was governed differently than a traditional British colony (such as those that would eventually become the United States). A protectorate is a territory that, while still under the influence and de facto rule of another state, is nominally allowed some degree of autonomy and self-rule on internal matters. A colony, by contrast, is a territory directly administered by the government of a foreign power. The British protectorate in Uganda also did not permit British citizens to hold land in the region, meaning there was no migration to or settlement in Uganda by the British. This is also in stark contrast to the colonial relationship, in which some degree of settlement from citizens of the ruling country is expected.

on the Baganda people in the south of the country. By contrast, the northern tribes were the source of most recruits to the armed forces and the local police. This had long-term effects on the region, since economic power came to be concentrated among the Bantu peoples of the south, while military power was concentrated in the north. This state of affairs persisted after Uganda received its independence, and even today many academic, governmental, and religious positions are held by Bantu people.

THE CHALLENGES OF INDEPENDENCE

Ugandans began agitating for independence in large numbers during the 1950s. The British had established a legislature for the protectorate in 1921, but it had initially been filled only with British citizens; the native Africans preferred the rule of their traditional tribal elders. This state of affairs was altered by World War II (1939—1945), during which the British had their attention drawn away from managing their empire and focused on the war in Europe. The people of Uganda began to take a more active role in the government as a result, and in the years following the war Africans began taking up seats on the Legislative Council. The one major holdout to participation in the colonial government was the kingdom of Buganda, which perceived the legislature as a threat to its power. Kabaka Mutesa II, the grandson of Mwanga II, followed

MILTON OBOTE

Born in 1925 in northern Uganda, Milton Obote was a member of the Lango ethnic group that had opposed the claim to power by the Baganda. He attended Makerere University in Kampala from 1948 to 1949, but was expelled for his political activism. He spent time in Kenya in the 1950s, where he became active in the struggle for Kenyan independence, and he brought the lessons he learned there back to Uganda with him. He was elected to the Legislative Council in 1958, where he was a vocal critic of the colonial government, and he was one of the founding members of the Uganda People's Congress (UPC) party. The UPC drew most of its support from the northern regions of the country and focused on limiting the power exerted by the southern kingdoms, most notably Buganda.

This monument in Kampala honors Mutesa II, the first president of Uganda after independence.

his ancestor's example by refusing to surrender his authority to the British and being briefly deposed as a result, only returning to power later as a constitutional ruler.

By the late 1950s, African political parties had begun to emerge, and a burgeoning independence movement was making demands of the British government. The kingdom of Buganda was also advocating for its own autonomy, separate from the rest of the protectorate. Between the devastation wrought by World War II and the growing independence movements in its various territories, the sun had finally begun to set on the British Empire. In the case of Uganda, the desire for independence brought about an African majority on the Legislative Council in 1961, prompting the start of formal negotiations in London to grant the protectorate its sovereignty. Uganda was given full independence on October 9, 1962. Kabaka Mutesa II was made president of the sovereign nation, while Milton Obote of the Uganda People's Congress (UPC) party was elected prime minister, a power-sharing agreement meant to unite the disparate ethnic factions within the country.

Obote advocated a new African sensibility, influenced by Jomo Kenyatta and other leaders of independence movements across the continent. His forward-looking embrace of Ugandan nationalism and socialism stood in stark opposition to Kabaka (and now President) Mutesa II, who had inherited his power from the colonial government and represented a continuation of that era. The ethnic and geographical divide between Obote and Mutesa II, the result of the borders carelessly drawn by the British decades before, also inflamed tensions within the new government. This tension simmered and eventually boiled over in 1966, when Obote suspended the constitution that had been drafted upon independence and ordered the arrest of the kabaka and several other government officials. Mutesa II fled the country and died in exile in 1969.

Obote assumed the presidency following Mutesa II's flight and enacted a new republican constitution. The most striking aspect of this new constitution was its abolition of the traditional tribal kingdoms. Obote wanted to bring Uganda into the modern era, ending systems of monarchy and promoting democracy across the nation. This move went over very poorly with the people formerly of the southern kingdoms, however, who had been largely happy with their traditional forms of government. Friction between Obote and the peoples and lands of the south increased over the next few years, and Obote began resorting to harsh tactics to repress his critics. Obote's efforts to nationalize key industries and distribute the profits among the Ugandan people led to widespread corruption and graft, further increasing the suspicions of many Ugandans toward their president. By the early 1970s, Obote's popularity was at an all-time low, and his promises of electoral reform were not enough to prevent the coup that removed him from power.

"To some European powers, Africa is their preserve and playing field. To them, no African government has the right to exercise self-determination."
—Milton Obote

UGANDA UNDER AMIN

In 1971, Obote was overthrown by his commander of the army, Idi Amin. Amin had been a crucial figure in Obote's government (he had led the attempt to arrest the kabaka in 1966), but his relationship with Obote had soured in the late 1960s due to political and ethnic differences. When Amin learned of his impending arrest for misappropriating military funds, he launched a

The unelected ruler of Uganda from 1971 to 1979, Idi Amin was born in the mid-1920s (the exact date is unknown) in the north of the country. A member of the Kakwa tribe, Amin was raised in poverty by his mother and did not receive any formal education. He took a job as a cook with the British colonial army to earn some money, and he was able to join the army as a soldier soon after. As a member of the King's African Rifles, he fought against the Mau Mau rebels in Kenya during the 1950s, and he was promoted several times, becoming one of the first Ugandan lieutenants in the regiment. He remained an important military figure after independence, eventually promoted to commander of the army. He was a longtime ally of Obote, but their relationship eventually fell apart in the late 1960s for reasons both political and personal. Amin began recruiting followers from among the Kakwa people, and the army itself became divided along ethnic lines, mirroring the rift between Amin and Obote. When Amin seized power in 1971, one of his first acts as president was to order the murders of any senior officers still loyal to Obote, in an effort to shore up his power.

long-planned coup, declaring himself president in January 1971, while Obote was out of the country. Amin's coup was welcomed by the Ugandan people, who believed the country would now finally be united. He was also embraced by the West, which had grown increasingly fearful of Obote's socialism and proposals to nationalize large, foreign-owned corporations. Amin promised a return to civilian government and seemed amenable to Western interests.

The optimism engendered by Amin's seizure of power was soon dispelled, however, as Amin became increasingly erratic and repressive. His promise to hold elections and restore democracy was swiftly abandoned, and in 1976 he declared himself "president for life." This rejection of popular rule was accompanied by outbursts of violence directed at any that opposed him, as well as a series of stunts designed to highlight his power and strength. He claimed to be the king of Scotland, awarded himself the Victoria Cross (the most prestigious decoration in the British armed forces), and forced Western officials to kneel or carry him on their shoulders. These self-aggrandizing gestures soon lost Amin whatever goodwill he had with Western powers.

Meanwhile, Amin's cruelty and violence eroded his support among Ugandans. Murder, destruction of property, looting, and rape increasingly became the hallmarks of his troops, and certain ethnicities were singled out for persecution. An economic crisis prompted by Amin's expulsion of the country's comparatively wealthy Asian residents only made matters worse. Initially sold as an attempt to return power and wealth to the Ugandan people, Amin's decision in 1972 to expel the South Asian population and seize their businesses and personal property was embraced by his people. It soon became apparent, however, that Amin's friends and associates were going to be given the bulk of the seized assets, and most of the businesses taken over were rapidly driven into the ground through mismanagement. Without the commercial expertise of, and services performed by, the Asian community, Uganda's economy collapsed. Black markets and personal farms soon became the only means of survival for many Ugandans.

With internal problems mounting, Amin launched an invasion of neighboring Tanzania in 1978, seizing its northern territories in an attempt to distract the population. The war proved disastrous for Amin, however, as Tanzanian troops were joined by Ugandan exiles, and together they were able to defeat Amin's army and launch a counter-invasion of Uganda. The coalition was victorious, and on April 11, 1979, Idi Amin was removed from power and forced to flee the

President Idi Amin wields a special baton of office and prominently displays his military decorations (including those he awarded to himself) while speaking at a rally circa 1976.

country. He lived the rest of his life in exile, eventually dying in Saudi Arabia in 2003. During his eight years in power, between three hundred thousand and four hundred thousand Ugandans were killed.

MUSEVENI COMES TO POWER

Following Amin's removal, a coalition government of former exiles, the Uganda National Liberation Front (UNLF), took power. The leadership of Uganda changed several times over the course of the next year, until Milton Obote won a highly contested election in December 1980. Obote had sought refuge in Tanzania when Amin had come to power, and he had shrewdly managed his position there, allowing for his return to the presidency a decade after he had been overthrown. His election was not widely supported, however, and he soon found himself dealing with multiple rebellions, including the National Resistance Movement (NRM) led by Yoweri Museveni.

Beginning with just twenty-six guns, Museveni's National Resistance Army (NRA), the military branch of the NRM, launched guerrilla attacks against Obote's government and was soon joined by other opponents of the administration. Obote tried and failed to restart the Ugandan economy, and he once again resorted to violence in an effort to maintain his position. He did nothing to stop reprisal killings against members of the Kakwa tribe, who were conflated with Amin in the minds of some Ugandans, and failed to win the support of the army. In 1985, Obote was deposed for a second time by officers from the Acholi tribe. Obote again fled the country, this time permanently. He died in South Africa in 2005, after his second stint as president cost the lives of one hundred thousand Ugandans. The National Resistance Movement defeated the Acholis who had deposed Obote, and in January 1986, Yoweri Museveni became president. He made peace with the remaining rebel groups in the country and invited them to join his government, ending five years of civil war.

MUSEVENI IN POWER

Museveni has remained president of Uganda since 1986, and he has achieved much during his three decades in power. He is primarily credited with restoring

Yoweri Kaguta Museveni was born in 1944 to a pastoral peasant family in Ankole, in the west of the country. The peasants in the region where he grew up received little in the way of education and health care, and were among the most exploited by British colonial policies, which forced them out of their traditional lands. In 1966, Museveni led a successful campaign in his village to encourage the peasants

to fence their land in and refuse to leave. He graduated from the University of Dar es Salaam in 1970 with a degree in economics and political science. While at university, he was part of a radical student group that met to discuss Pan-Africanism and anticolonial politics; many of his classmates would go on to become influential political figures across Africa. Museveni opposed Amin's dictatorship and was part of the army that removed him from power. He served in various positions in the post-Amin governments and was also opposed to Obote coming back to power. He vowed that if Obote rigged the December 1980 election, he would refuse to accept the result and would lead a guerrilla struggle. When this appeared to be the case, Museveni kept his word, launching the National Resistance Movement (NRM) in 1981.

political and economic stability to a country ravaged by fifteen years of dictatorship and civil war. A new constitution was drafted by a Constituent Assembly in 1995, and Museveni deliberately refused to speak on specific issues related to its development, to make sure it was recognized as a legitimate source of legal authority and not as a document codifying one particular president's power. His efforts paid off, and the constitution has held for more than two decades, with elections occurring at regular five-year intervals. Museveni has sought to bridge gaps between Ugandan citizens, restoring personal freedoms revoked by Amin or Obote, and has maintained discipline in the military. He has also reversed the most controversial policies of his predecessors. The

The Lord's Resistance Army (LRA), led by Joseph Kony (shown here), posed a serious internal security threat to Uganda in the years following Museveni's rise to power.

traditional tribal kingdoms, abolished by Obote, were once again officially recognized in 1993. Though still subject to the oversight of the elected government, the tribal kingdoms do have some degree of internal autonomy. The government also formally invited the expelled Asian community to return in the 1990s, with property restored to those it was taken from wherever possible. Regional cooperation has been developed between Uganda, Kenya, Tanzania, Rwanda, and Burundi, with the implementation of a common market and many shared services. Museveni has also cultivated strong relationships with powers in the West and East, and has secured enough foreign investment in Uganda to restore the economy to a degree of stability. The wealth being generated, however, is largely extracted by those same investors, and ordinary Ugandans often work for only dollars a day. In this respect, Uganda's relationship with its investors is in some ways indistinguishable from the imperial relationship with the British.

Museveni's rule has not been without its problems. Though security has improved for most of the country, the flood of arms unleashed by the civil war in the 1980s eventually made its way to various antigovernment groups. The most dangerous of these was the Lord's Resistance Army (LRA), established in the late 1980s by Joseph Kony. Ostensibly attempting to install a government based on the Ten Commandments, the LRA spent twenty years attacking civilians in northern Uganda, terrorizing and displacing nearly two million people. The LRA also abducted tens of thousands of children, forcing them to work as either slaves or soldiers. Peace talks were attempted several times in the mid-2000s but inevitably broke down. In 2008, Uganda began a joint military operation with the Democratic Republic of the Congo (DRC) and South Sudan, targeting LRA bases in the DRC. Though Kony evaded capture, the group was weakened and driven out of Uganda. After several further years of searching, the LRA was deemed to be so weak that, according to the Ugandan army, "[Kony] no longer poses any significant threat to Uganda's security." Kony is still wanted on war crimes charges from the International Criminal Court. Uganda has also faced terrorism from the Somalia-based group al-Shabaab, perpetrated in retaliation for Ugandan participation in African Union activities carried out against the group. Though these attacks have been limited in scope, Museveni has consistently raised the military budget in response.

More worryingly for Uganda's future, however, is Museveni's reluctance to give up power, and the increasingly antidemocratic measures he is taking to maintain his position. Self-described "president for life" Idi Amin was in power for less than ten years; Museveni has passed the three-decade mark and shows no signs of stepping down anytime soon. Though he has been elected at regular five-year intervals since coming to power, his victories have not been without controversy. For many years, multiparty politics were effectively banned in the country, meaning Museveni's election was largely ceremonial. When a referendum passed in 2005, opening up the political system in the country, it was tied to a lifting of the constitutional restriction on the number of terms a president could serve. Museveni's subsequent elections in 2006, 2011, and 2016 have all come under scrutiny from both international observers and opposition politicians. It has become common for Museveni's opponents to be arrested and imprisoned in the weeks or months preceding elections, preventing them from campaigning. Police and military deployments have also been used as intimidation tactics, and areas of the country in which opposition parties are concentrated are often missing election materials and experience voting irregularities. Social media sites, including Facebook and Twitter, were shut down on election day in 2016, a last-ditch attempt to suppress the vote that prompted a concerned phone call from US secretary of state John Kerry.

Despite condemnations from around the world of Ugandan electoral processes, Museveni is only accelerating his attempts to hold on to power. The Parliament, controlled by Museveni's NRM party, voted in 2017 to remove the age restriction on presidential candidates, allowing Museveni to stand for election again in 2021. The country was also the subject of international condemnation when pop-star-turned-politician Robert Kyagulanyi Ssentamu, also known as Bobi Wine, was arrested and tortured by Ugandan police in 2018. Elected to Parliament himself in 2017, Kyagulanyi was campaigning

Robert Kyagulanyi, also known as Bobi Wine, was elected to Parliament in 2017. He has attracted a significant level of support for his criticisms of President Museveni. Here he delivers a speech in 2018.

for an opposition candidate in a special election at the time of his arrest. Kyagulanyi has been an outspoken critic of Museveni, and his popularity in Uganda, particularly among the young, has made him a credible challenger for the presidency in 2021, a fact likely to be at least partially responsible for his detention and mistreatment. Protests in support of Kyagulanyi have been violently broken up by the police, and dozens of protesters have been arrested.

In the coming years, protecting Uganda's young democracy will be one of the greatest challenges faced by the country. Museveni himself came to power after launching a war to topple a president he viewed as illegitimate, and the increasingly antidemocratic tactics he has used to maintain his position now risk provoking a similar revolt. Such violence would jeopardize all that Uganda has achieved in the last thirty years and would have its worst effects on the

> ## REFUGEES IN UGANDA

Uganda is the largest host of refugees in Africa and currently the third-largest in the world. Well over one million refugees have been admitted into Uganda, mostly from South Sudan. Two thousand South Sudanese refugees have arrived daily since July 2016, fleeing violence in their homeland. These are in addition to the nearly three hundred thousand refugees displaced by fighting in the Democratic Republic of the Congo. Other sources of displaced persons include Rwanda, Burundi, and Somalia.

country's most vulnerable people. The effort to maintain self-governance within Uganda is also matched by the broader struggle to realize a meaningful independence on the world stage. Though no longer formally a part of the British Empire, Uganda remains, like most of its African neighbors, a source of wealth for the world's powers. Until Uganda's citizens receive the material benefits realized from the extraction of resources and labor from their country, the shadow of imperialism will remain.

INTERNET LINKS

https://www.britannica.com/place/Uganda
The Encyclopedia Britannica entry for Uganda presents not only a comprehensive overview of the nation's history but also information about the country's economy, geography, and population.

http://thecommonwealth.org/our-member-countries/uganda/history
This website contains information about the history of Uganda.

GOVERNMENT

President Yoweri Museveni gives an address at the State House in Entebbe in 2018.

3

THE GOVERNMENT OF UGANDA consists of three branches: the executive, the legislative, and the judicial. The country is a presidential republic, in which citizens vote for representatives in a national Parliament and for the president. The current system of government has only existed since Yoweri Museveni came to power in 1986, and the latest constitution was adopted on September 27, 1995. This makes Uganda's democracy a very young one, and it is fragile as a result. Increasingly antidemocratic tactics have been used in recent years by Museveni to maintain his power, and the government has struggled to combat corruption and establish justice.

THE PRESIDENCY

The executive branch of Uganda is led by the president, Yoweri Kaguta Museveni. The president is both the head of state and the head of government in Uganda, as well as the chief of the armed forces. The president is assisted by a prime minister and a cabinet, whom he or she appoints to their posts. The cabinet is made up of either current members of the Parliament or of people who meet the qualifications for election to the legislative body. The president is elected by absolute majority of the popular vote; if no candidate receives a majority in the first round of balloting, the two candidates who received the highest number of votes go into a run-off election. All Ugandans over the age of eighteen are eligible to vote. The president is elected to a five-year term, and as of 2005, there is no limit on the number of terms a president may serve.

The revocation of term limits is part of a broader problem faced by the Ugandan people, namely the president's gradual attempts to turn his office into a lifelong position. The constitution of 1995 initially established a "no-party" system of government, giving Museveni's National Resistance Movement (NRM) party complete power over the Parliament and the presidency. It was

The State House in Entebbe is one of two official residences of the president. The other is in the capital city of Kampala.

THE COMPOSITION OF THE TENTH PARLIAMENT

Uganda's tenth Parliament, elected in February 2016, contains 445 seats. Their distribution is as follows:

- *290 constituent representatives*
- *112 special female representatives*
- *10 representatives for the Uganda Peoples' Defence Forces*
- *5 representatives for the youth*
- *5 representatives for persons with disabilities*
- *5 representatives for workers*
- *18 ex officio members*

only in 2005 that a referendum allowing for multiparty democracy passed with overwhelming public support. In exchange for allowing other parties to compete in elections, Museveni had the imposition of term limits on the president done away with. In 2017, his party also passed a measure through Parliament lifting the age limit for holding presidential office, another barrier that would have removed him from power. Opposition parties have also been harshly cracked down on during elections, with both politicians and their supporters arrested and beaten by forces loyal to Museveni. Though Uganda is a democratic country on paper, in reality, the government is becoming increasingly dictatorial and resistant to meaningful public oversight.

THE PARLIAMENT

The legislative branch of Uganda consists of the Parliament, a unicameral body of 445 representatives that debates and passes laws to govern the country. Most (402) members of Parliament are elected by simple majority vote and serve for five-year terms. Elections for Parliament occur on the same cycle as elections for the presidency. Both Museveni and the current Parliament (the tenth in Uganda's history) were last elected in 2016; the next elections will be in 2021. As a result of the years when multiple political parties were prevented from contesting elections, Museveni's NRM party established an

President Museveni (*at podium*) addresses a session of Parliament, the legislative body of Uganda.

iron grip over the Parliament that it still maintains today. Even a decade after the introduction of multiparty politics, the NRM holds nearly three hundred seats in the Parliament, giving it a commanding majority.

A unique feature of Uganda's Parliament is its inclusion of reserved seats for representatives of particular institutions and interest groups. Each administrative district of Uganda is allowed to elect one female candidate to the Parliament, in addition to any other women who win constituency elections, to ensure that women's interests and voices are represented. As a result, women hold approximately 35 percent of the seats in the legislature. The Parliament also contains special places for representatives of the armed forces, workers, youth, and persons with disabilities, to be appointed by the president. Finally, cabinet ministers that are not elected members of the Parliament are allowed to sit in on the body's sessions and participate in discussions, but they are not allowed to cast votes. These are known as ex officio members.

LOCAL AND TRIBAL ADMINISTRATION

Uganda is composed of 121 districts spread across four administrative regions: Northern, Eastern, Central, and Western. Most districts are named after their main commercial or administrative town. Each district is further divided into subdistricts and counties, which are themselves made up of parishes and villages. The head elected official in a district is the chairperson of the local council.

Parallel with the state administration, five traditional Bantu kingdoms have remained, enjoying some degree of mainly cultural autonomy. Before the arrival of the British, the social structure of the region centered around tribal groupings. The members of a tribe chose their own leaders and made their own laws, which all members of the group were expected to follow. This method of self-governance remained important, particularly to the members of the southern tribal kingdoms, long after the British came to power, and Milton Obote's abolition of the traditional tribal kingdoms in 1967 was a major contributing factor to his fall from power. The rights of the kingdoms were restored by Yoweri Museveni in 1993.

THE JUDICIARY AND CRIMINAL JUSTICE

The judicial branch of Uganda's government consists of the Supreme Court, the most powerful in the country, as well as a number of lower-level courts. The Supreme Court is made up of a chief justice and at least six other associate justices. Supreme Court justices are appointed by the president and approved by the Parliament. Justices are not allowed to serve past the age of seventy.

The justice system in Uganda is plagued by serious problems. The police have been granted an incredible amount of discretion in their ability to break up public and private gatherings, often dispersing peaceful assemblies and protests. Political opponents of the NRM are regularly arrested, and security officials are accustomed to using excessive force. Over one hundred people, including several children, were killed in one particularly brutal crackdown in November 2016. Torture, despite being illegal under Ugandan law, is regularly used by the police and armed forces against prisoners, and can range from beatings to electric shocks and submersion underwater. In 2016, one billion shillings ($275,000 US) were awarded as compensation to people who had been tortured by the state, though many defendants have claimed they never received the money. Police and military officials are rarely held accountable for their abuses of power, and vacancies in the court system slow down the application of justice, preventing detainees from bringing abuses to light. Prisons are overcrowded and understaffed, many detainees are not charged before being imprisoned, and bribery of judges ensures that certain defendants are denied anything resembling justice.

Ugandan women also face an extra level of gender-based discrimination and violence. Though rape and domestic violence are illegal, the wording of these laws creates enough loopholes that the criminal justice system is unable to help

According to police statistics, gender-based violence increased by 4 percent from 2015 to 2016 alone. Considering that many incidents of such violence are never reported, this is an understatement of the problem.

many victims. Women are discriminated against in employment, education, marriage, divorce, inheritance, and owning property. Sexual harassment is a common problem for Ugandan women of all classes, including female members of Parliament. Sexual assault and rape are also regular occurrences, with 22 percent of women aged fifteen to forty-nine reporting experiencing some form of sexual violence in a 2016 survey. Women report being assaulted by employers, police officers, teachers, religious leaders, and intimate partners. Since spousal rape is not accounted for under Ugandan law, the latter category of abusers is often not subject to prosecution. Few rapes are reported overall, as women fear the stigma and potential legal consequences that will follow if they come forward. Domestic violence is also a growing problem. More than half of all women in Uganda report having experienced violence from an intimate partner, and there were 50 percent more women killed in instances of domestic violence in 2016 than in 2010. Domestic violence is much more common in rural areas and among women with less education, though its effects are

The rise in gender-based violence and the lack of official justice have prompted many Ugandans to take to the streets in protest. Here, women are protesting against violence against women.

felt at all levels of society. In February 2018, Susan Magara, the daughter of a wealthy businessman, was kidnapped and killed, one of more than twenty women whose bodies have been dumped on the streets of Kampala since the start of 2017. Ambassadors from France and the United States joined Ugandan demonstrators in protesting the rising level of violence against women and demanding answers from the government.

The lack of investigation and follow-up to issues involving women is symptomatic of the broader malady affecting the government. Ugandans feel the police are ineffective at addressing crime because they are spending the majority of their time attacking opponents of the president. This attitude is supported by the facts—Robert Kyagulanyi (Bobi Wine) was prevented from performing concerts in October 2017 while an investigation into his lyrics was carried out, and Makerere University professor Stella Nyanzi was arrested for cyber harassment after calling the president "a pair of buttocks" on Facebook. The seriousness with which these moments of political expression were taken, contrasted with the lack of urgency into investigating murders and rapes, is revealing of the government's priorities. Museveni's desire to hold on to power, and his use of the police to pursue that desire, draws resources away from people and parts of the country that desperately need them. The increasingly undemocratic nature of Uganda's government is not simply a matter of electoral dominance by one party, but a meaningful restriction on the ability of the vast majority of the Ugandan populace to achieve justice.

INTERNET LINKS

http://www.statehouse.go.ug
The official website for the executive branch of the Ugandan government contains information about the government's structure, as well as biographical details about the president and his top officials.

https://ulii.org/ug/legislation/consolidated-act/0
The Ugandan constitution of 1995 is the founding legal document of the current government.

ECONOMY

The growth, harvest, and export of coffee beans, harvested from the coffee fruit (shown here), is the backbone of the Ugandan economy and provides employment for many Ugandan citizens.

4

THE UGANDAN ECONOMY HAS MADE significant strides over the last thirty years. Thanks in large part to foreign assistance, the economy has achieved a degree of long-term stability. Growth averaged 8 percent a year between 1992 and 2010, tripling per capita GDP and significantly reducing poverty. Since then, however, growth has slowed and investment has plateaued. A return to a vibrant economy depends on many factors outside the control of the government. The Ugandan economy is heavily based on foreign exchange, with agriculture accounting for the bulk of exports and providing the most jobs. Fishing and industry are also important, while tourism brings substantial revenue for the country. Still, life for many Ugandans is incredibly difficult, and poverty remains a fact of life for the majority of Ugandan citizens.

"The NRM and other reformers before it had to trigger socio-economic transformation that would see our mainly peasant society ... metamorphose into a middle-class and skilled working-class society."
–President Yoweri Museveni

AN ECONOMIC SLOWDOWN

Uganda's economy improved rapidly during the 1990s and 2000s, as a result of heavy foreign investment and the government's adherence to neoliberal economic policies. The implementation of austerity programs qualified the country for debt relief in 1997, and the economy continued to grow even during the global economic recession of 2007—2009. Since that time, however, the growth rate has dropped by nearly 50 percent, and the country's economy has stagnated. Foreign investment in the country began to taper off, partly due to the recession but also as a result of regional factors, among them increasing violence across East Africa, poor returns on investment, and crises resulting from climate change. A massive drought in the Horn of Africa has been the most obvious climate-related disaster in the region, but changes in rainfall patterns have also wreaked havoc on the Ugandan economy, which is reliant on agricultural exports.

While the economy has not collapsed, its ability to resume steady growth is dependent on several variables beyond Ugandan control. Revenues from oil reserves discovered in 2006 are expected to start offsetting some of the country's debt over the next decade, but only if the income generated matches what is expected. The reliance on rain-fed agriculture will also pose a risk going forward as the effects of climate change get more severe. Regional conflicts and another global trade slowdown are also not outside the realm of possibility, nor is the idea that investments could begin drying up if public projects are not executed properly. Overall, while Uganda is endowed with significant natural resources, and while both oil exploration and infrastructure projects are poised to drive growth over the next few years, economic prosperity is by no means a sure thing, and a further economic downturn could just as easily be on the horizon.

COMPONENTS OF THE ECONOMY

Of the many sectors of the Ugandan economy, agriculture is by far the most important. Agricultural land accounts for 71 percent of the total land use in the country, and 71 percent of the workforce is employed in the agricultural

MONEY MATTERS

The basic unit of currency in Uganda is the shilling. Issuance of currency is overseen by the Bank of Uganda, the country's central banking institution. One US dollar is worth approximately 3,760 Ugandan shillings as of 2018. Ugandan currency consists of banknotes and coins. Coins are used for denominations of 1,000 shillings or less, while banknotes range from

1,000 shillings to 50,000 shillings. The notes depict elements of Uganda's natural and cultural history, including a map of the country, Ugandan basketry and mat patterns, a man wearing a traditional tribal headdress, and the Independence Monument in Kampala. Varieties of Ugandan wildlife are also pictured on several of the notes.

sector. Twenty-eight percent of Uganda's gross domestic product (GDP) comes from agriculture, and agricultural products supply nearly all of Uganda's foreign exchange earnings. Coffee is the number-one export in the country, accounting for 16 percent of all exports and making Uganda the second-biggest coffee producer in all of Africa (behind only Ethiopia). Other major agricultural exports include tea, cotton, tobacco, cassava, potatoes, millet, and corn.

Uganda has an ideal climate and extremely rich soil for growing crops, but changes in rainfall patterns as a result of climate change in the twentieth and twenty-first centuries have disrupted many farmers' harvests. Since so much of the economy is dependent on agriculture, this could pose a massive challenge for the country in the years to come should conditions such as droughts become more prevalent.

In addition to the growing of various crops, Ugandan farmers also raise a variety of livestock. Cattle, sheep, and goats are the most common, followed by pigs, chickens, ducks, and turkeys. There is also a growing dairy industry in the country.

The mining of gold is a laborious job, but the precious metal contributes significantly to the Ugandan economy.

Manufacturing accounts for 23 percent of Uganda's GDP, and the manufacturing sector plays an important role in adding value to agricultural output by producing food and beverages from raw foodstuffs. Domestically produced consumer goods include plastics, soap, cork, beer, and soft drinks. Uganda also derives income from sugar processing and the production of cotton textiles, steel, and cement. Further growth in the industrial sector is hampered by Uganda's dependence on imports, as well as the country's lack of infrastructure.

Mining is also an important sector of the Ugandan economy. Interest in Uganda's mineral potential increased substantially following improvements in the country's mining and investment regulation. According to World Bank figures, between 2003 and 2007 mining revenues in Uganda grew by 202 percent, from $550,000 in 2003 to $1.66 million in 2007. Gold accounts for 10 percent of Uganda's total exports and has benefited from the deregulation of gold sales by the central bank. There are also small deposits of tin in the south of the country, as well as sources of copper and cobalt.

Fishing is of growing importance in Uganda. Lakes, rivers, and swamps cover 10.9 million acres (4.4 million hectares), and fish contribute a high proportion of Uganda's protein needs. The private sector has taken a great interest in fisheries and has developed facilities for fish farming, fish processing, and the export trade, supported by the government and Chinese investors. There is a danger of overfishing, however, especially in the Lake Kyoga region.

Lake Victoria, together with the many other lakes found in Uganda, provides excellent fishing opportunities for the Ugandan people.

Finally, tourism plays an important role in generating foreign exchange, high-end employment, and investment. Tourism was the third-leading source of foreign exchange in the years before Idi Amin came to power but was rendered nearly nonexistent during his dictatorship and the civil war that followed. Increased investment in travel accommodations and related facilities in the twenty-first century has rejuvenated the industry. Adventure tourism, ecotourism, and cultural tourism are all being developed, with the country's national parks and endangered wildlife being the largest attractions. About three-quarters of Uganda's tourists are from other African countries, most notably the bordering nation of Kenya. Other visitors arrive from Europe, the United Kingdom, and the United States each year.

ENERGY AND OIL

Renewable resources provide much of the energy in Uganda as part of a government push to become energy self-sufficient. There is a long way yet to go, however, as only 22 percent of the population has access to electricity, a figure that drops to 10 percent in rural areas. Even those with electricity experience frequent power cuts, called load shedding, and Uganda imports some of its electric power from neighboring Kenya. Of the power generated within Uganda, about 68 percent comes from hydroelectric plants. In particular, the capacity of the Nalubaale Power Station (formerly Owen Falls Dam) on the Victoria Nile is now 380 megawatts.

Uganda's days as an energy-importing country may be near an end, however. Oil was struck in 2006, with reserves of 6.5 billion barrels discovered in the area around Lake Albert. Foreign money has flooded into the country as a result, with the China National Offshore Oil Corporation (CNOOC) the biggest investor. British and French companies are also involved, and initial development work has begun. Investors have earmarked $9 billion for production facilities, $2 billion to $3 billion more for a refinery, and $3.5 billion for a pipeline. A deal was reached in 2017 to run an 898-mile (1,445 km) pipeline through Tanzania to the Indian Ocean seaport of Tanga, and the ground was later cleared for the construction of a new airport to transport personnel and equipment to the oil-rich region of the country. Oil production is expected to begin in 2020 or 2021, and the Ugandan government is anticipating significant revenue generation. On the other hand, if something were to delay the project, or if less oil is produced than expected, the country's financial outlook would be significantly altered. If all goes according to plan, Uganda would be the first East African nation to export crude oil.

LABOR IN UGANDA

Uganda's labor force consists of approximately 15.8 million people, 71 percent of whom work in agriculture. Service workers make up another 22 percent, with 7 percent employed in industrial jobs. While the official unemployment rate is around 9 percent, more than three-quarters of Ugandan workers earn their living through "vulnerable" employment, jobs that could vanish at any moment. Poverty is common in Uganda, where 34 percent of the population lives in extreme poverty (defined as living on less than $1.90 US per day). While the number of people in such circumstances has decreased over the last fifteen years, it is still an unacceptably high number, and it obscures how easy it is for a person to fall back into poverty. Many Ugandans who make enough money to no longer count as extremely poor do so thanks to a good harvest and good prices for their crops; if the weather turns against them a year later, they can fall right back into poverty. Extreme poverty is

THE AFRICAN ECONOMIC COMMUNITY

Uganda is a member of the African Economic Community (AEC). This organization of African Union states established grounds for mutual economic development among the majority of African nations. The stated goals of the organization include the creation of free trade areas, customs unions, a single market, a central bank, and a common currency, thus establishing an economic and monetary union. While progress toward these goals has been sporadic around the continent, the East African Community (EAC) of Uganda, Tanzania, Kenya, Rwanda, Burundi, and South Sudan has established a free trade area and a customs union. The EAC is also part of the broader African Free Trade Zone (AFTZ), a free trade bloc of twenty-six countries.

concentrated in the agricultural regions of the north and east of the country, where 84 percent of those living below the poverty line reside. Women are also more vulnerable than men, as women in Uganda make less money, experience higher unemployment, and are significantly underrepresented in the non-agricultural workforce.

The minimum wage in Uganda is less than $2 US per month, and efforts to push the government into raising it have so far had little success. Protections for workers are also scant. Terminations and termination payments are regulated by law, but employers are also allowed to fire an employee with no benefits if he or she "fundamentally violates his or her terms of employment," a phrase vague enough to cover nearly anything. Unions are allowed in the private sector, but not in most parts of the public sector. Since most Ugandans work in agriculture or in other forms of informal labor, and the largest single employer is the government, this means that the vast majority of Ugandan laborers have no access to a union (though union officials estimate that nearly half of those working in a job with a union are members). Working conditions are also unsafe for many Ugandans due to poor enforcement of existing laws or simply to the nature of agricultural and informal work. Less than one-third of all workers have secondary education or vocational training,

Agriculture, including the planting of rice, provides employment for the majority of Ugandans.

In Uganda, 30 percent of children between the ages of five and fourteen are working in some capacity. The vast majority work in the agricultural sector, helping their parents tend fields, harvest crops, and scare off pests. Others work in the cities, selling plastic bags or scrap metal, or simply begging. The most abusive forms of child labor include quarrying stone, mining,

and forced prostitution. Most child laborers work to supplement their family's income (45 percent of households living below the poverty line have children working), and the money they earn is often used to pay school fees for themselves or their siblings. Only 34 percent of child laborers manage to maintain some kind of balance between school and work; most are forced to drop out. A 2016 law criminalized the hiring of children under the age of fourteen, but it has not stopped exploitation, as two million children across Uganda are still estimated to be working. Many children are unaware of how to go about reporting their situations to the authorities, and there are not enough inspectors in the country to follow up on all reported cases. The law also calls for the arrest of the parents of working children, an overly punitive response that will only worsen the problem, as children will now be even less financially secure than they were before. To meaningfully address the problem of child labor, Uganda will need an ambitious program aimed at eliminating poverty for all Ugandans; the current laws and programs in place do not go far enough toward this end.

though a small fraction have received training to work in the oil sector from the Uganda Petroleum Institute since its opening in 2010. Employers are required to contribute an amount equal to 10 percent of an employee's gross salary to the National Social Security Fund (NSSF), and an additional 5 percent is deducted from the employee's salary for the fund.

TRANSPORTATION INFRASTRUCTURE

The transportation infrastructure in Uganda suffered heavily during the period of civil unrest. Roads and railways were destroyed during the years of dictatorship and civil war, and it has taken decades to recover. Though the government has made improvements to the transportation infrastructure a priority, it has also failed to invest in local engineering firms, instead developing business relationships with China that are neocolonial in nature.

Motorbike taxis, popularly called *boda bodas*, are the most popular form of transportation in Uganda. They hold a driver and as many as three other

Boda boda motorbikes can carry multiple passengers, but they can also be dangerous.

people—too many for one bike. *Boda bodas* are somewhat dangerous, too, as many of the drivers are inexperienced and drive recklessly. Other common modes of transportation include special-hire taxis, minivans, bicycles, or old-fashioned walking.

There are 16,650 miles (26,800 km) of road in Uganda, 23 percent of them paved. Most of the country's damaged highway network has been repaired since the end of the civil war, and new motorways are being constructed. The vast majority of contracts for these road repairs have gone to Chinese companies, however, a fact that has raised objections from many Ugandans. Of the forty-eight road projects initiated between 2008 and 2018, 70 percent were awarded to Chinese contractors. More than half of the funding for these projects came directly from the Ugandan government, and Ugandan engineers have pointed out that that money could have been better invested in local firms, where it would have gone back into the Ugandan economy. A law aimed at establishing preferential policies for local firms and workers (versions of which exist in neighboring countries such as Kenya, Rwanda, and Tanzania) was passed in 2017 and then swiftly repealed by the Parliament in February 2018. Calls to restore the law have been ignored. Without such legislation, Chinese firms are able to register in Uganda and bid on projects immediately, undercutting local competition. This is part of a broader push by China to extend its influence into East Africa; Chinese firms have invested in major construction projects across

The expressway connecting Kampala with Entebbe International Airport is one example of a new piece of transportation infrastructure in Uganda built by Chinese firms.

the region and have provided hundreds of millions of dollars in economic aid to Uganda. Infrastructure projects across Uganda have been either carried out by Chinese firms or underwritten by loans from Chinese banks, fostering a relationship that has echoes of British imperialism. Ugandan wealth is not being distributed among the Ugandan people, many of whom desperately need it—instead, it's going to foreign investors and corporations.

Chinese investment and construction were not only responsible for building a new four-lane highway connecting Kampala with Entebbe International Airport, they were also crucial to expansions at the airport itself. Today, Uganda has forty-seven airports.

Uganda's railroad system consists of 773 miles (1,244 km) of track, most of which runs between stations within the country. There is only one international linkage via rail, with Kenya. The Uganda Railways Corporation (URC) provides passenger and freight services.

Most of the major lakes in Uganda have ferry services that crisscross the water and link any small islands to the mainland. Lake Victoria sees the most commercial traffic. In conjunction with train services, the railway companies of Uganda and Tanzania operate train ferries on the lake between railhead ports in both countries and Kenya. These ferries load rail coaches and wagons. River transport is very limited in Uganda, as there are few navigable stretches in the country. Only parts of the Albert Nile receive some traffic.

INTERNET LINKS

https://www.afdb.org/en/countries/east-africa/uganda
The African Development Bank Group gives an overview of the Ugandan economy, including the challenges it currently faces and its likely future prospects.

http://www.worldbank.org/en/country/uganda/overview
The World Bank not only provides information on Uganda's current economic outlook, it also details the results of the work it has undertaken within the country.

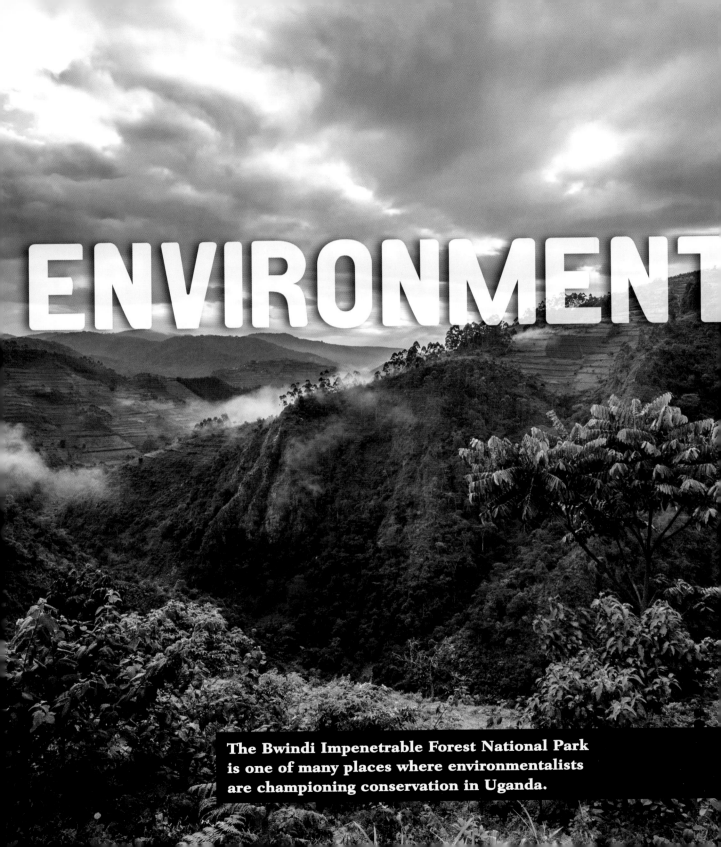

ENVIRONMENT

The Bwindi Impenetrable Forest National Park is one of many places where environmentalists are championing conservation in Uganda.

5

UGANDA IS A COUNTRY OF abundant natural resources and breathtaking raw beauty. Its environmental bounty is under threat, however, from a variety of sources. Climate change has already had a profound impact on Uganda, and its effects are going to be felt for decades to come. Deforestation has led to increased flooding and disease, and air pollution poses a major public health crisis. The draining of wetlands, pollution of water, and poaching of rare animals are also ongoing problems. The government has taken steps to address these issues, investing in renewable resources and taking steps to protect the country's air, land, and endangered species, but more will need to be done to prevent further environmental degradation.

"Over the last, say, twenty years, the rain pattern has completely changed. Rain comes at a time when you don't expect it. Sunshine or drought come at a time when you should be having rain." –Sam Massa, coffee farmer

CLIMATE CHANGE

Climate change has produced heavy downpours in Uganda in recent years, resulting in flooding that washes out roads and destroys crops.

Of the many challenges facing Uganda's environment, arguably the most significant and potentially devastating is climate change. The effects of Earth's rising temperatures and shifting climate patterns have been felt in Uganda, as well as in East Africa as a whole, in the twenty-first century. The average annual temperature has increased by 0.2 degrees Celsius (0.36 degrees Fahrenheit) per decade since the 1980s, and the rate of increase is expected to rise in the future. Some experts predict that the country could be 2 degrees hotter by midcentury than it is now. Climate change has also had a major impact on rainfall in Uganda, making its timing far more unpredictable. The stable wet seasons that have characterized Uganda for centuries are becoming more erratic, with long periods of drought punctuated by sudden downpours. The unusually heavy periods of rainfall lead to flooding—in late 2007, tens of thousands of people were displaced by one such downpour.

The extended periods of drought are potentially even more harmful, as they threaten the agricultural production so many Ugandans rely on for their livelihoods. The coffee trees that one in five Ugandans depend on for part or all of their income are particularly sensitive to temperature shifts and droughts, which make them less productive and more susceptible to pests and disease. Since most coffee harvesting is carried out by small farmers with no access to irrigation or modern agricultural production, a single bad crop can be devastating. Farmers and their families are forced to go without food and medicine, and their children are driven out of schools to try to find some form of work. According to one analysis commissioned by the Ugandan government, climate change could cut domestic coffee production in half by 2050, representing a loss of $1.2 billion and spelling disaster for millions of rural Ugandans. This problem is widespread across East Africa, where extended droughts have resulted in famine conditions for millions of people.

Uganda is taking climate change seriously. While the country's carbon footprint is almost zero, the government has signed on to the Paris Climate

Agreement, proposed in 2015, and is attempting to boost its renewable energy production. Though the vast majority of the country's energy consumption already comes from renewable sources, public and private investments in hydroelectric, solar, and geothermal energy are on the rise in an effort to make the country as environmentally friendly as possible. This commitment to combating climate change is complicated by the government's eager anticipation of revenues generated from oil drilling, a contradiction that will likely receive greater scrutiny in the future.

The white rhinoceros is one of several endangered animals protected within Uganda's national parks.

DEFORESTATION AND CONSERVATION

Forests cover approximately 10.4 percent of Uganda's surface area as of 2018, a 56 percent reduction since 1990. The country loses an average of 212,511 acres (86,000 ha) of trees each year. Most of this destruction takes place on private land, outside of government-protected areas. Forests are cleared for timber and to make room for farmland, but the loss of so many trees has major environmental consequences. Deforestation prevents water retention in the soil during heavy downpours, leading to increased flooding that destroys homes, businesses, and crops. The flooding also increases waterborne diseases, including cholera, which affect Ugandans of all ages. Extensive deforestation contributes to climate change, too, as there are fewer trees to absorb carbon dioxide from the air.

Uganda is also home to nearly fifty species of endangered mammals, reptiles, and birds, as well as a number of rare plants. The gorillas of the southwestern mountains are the rarest of these creatures, which also include endangered rhinoceroses, elephants, and the Nile crocodile. In an effort to preserve the country's forests and the animals that live within them, ten national parks have been established throughout Uganda, under the control of the Uganda Wildlife Authority (UWA). Despite these efforts, poachers remain a problem, whether they are hunting for sport, food, or profit, and more rangers are likely necessary to properly monitor the parks.

The number of vehicles in Uganda has quadrupled since 1971, leading to a similarly massive increase in outdoor air pollution. This problem is particularly acute in major cities, including the capital, Kampala, where poor health outcomes are often at least partially linked to polluted air. Air pollution contributes to chronic lung diseases, including bronchial asthma, and could lead to lung cancer. Studies conducted in Kampala have found that 14 percent of children between the ages of eight and fourteen have bronchial asthma. Increased emissions standards for vehicles have been pointed to as one way in which air quality can be improved; reducing the number of cars on the roads by encouraging public transportation or walking has also been suggested. Combating air pollution is difficult, however, because it is not an immediately visible problem. Unlike damaged roads or sanitation infrastructure, polluted air cannot be seen and does not have an immediate impact on the day-to-day life of Ugandans. This makes it a lower priority for the Ugandan government, which has done little beyond encouraging the education of the populace about lung diseases caused by air pollution. In rural areas, air pollution is generated by the burning of firewood and charcoal indoors. This is an issue that mostly affects Uganda's poor, who use these sources of fuel for cooking. Improved stoves and renewable energy sources have been suggested as solutions to this problem, and many rural dwellings have been able to convert to more modern cooking appliances.

THE WETLANDS

Uganda's varied wetlands, which include grass swamps, mountain bogs, seasonal floodplains, and swamp forests, are a vital contributor to the national economy. They provide services and products worth hundreds of millions of dollars per year, and many Ugandans depend on the country's wetlands for their livelihoods. The wetlands are a source of water, construction material, and fuel, and can be used for farming, fishing, and grazing livestock. Wetlands supply direct or subsistence employment for nearly three million people, almost 10 percent of the population. In many parts of the country, wetland products and services act as a safety net for the poorest households.

This makes the degradation of the wetlands a major problem for many people. Several wetlands have been drained for agricultural use, and others have been severely polluted. In the district of Kampala, some wetlands have been turned into dumping sites for waste products from factories and garages. Furthermore, whenever it rains, additional polluting materials are carried into the wetlands. Even those that are connected to major bodies of water, including Lake Victoria and Lake Kyoga, have been heavily contaminated by both industrial and domestic waste. When these pollutants enter wetlands where crops are grown, they are extracted and absorbed by the crops. Although it is illegal to grow food on some of the Kampala wetlands, the ever-increasing population in the city has forced some Ugandans to reside in those areas, where they risk exposing their crops to contamination.

Wetlands are an important part of the Ugandan economy but are at risk of being severely degraded by pollution.

WATER AND SANITATION

While Uganda has more than enough sources of freshwater within its borders, its distribution is uneven. Nearly twenty-four million people lack access to clean water, particularly in rural areas. Improved water is more readily available in the cities, but rapid population growth in urban areas has put increasing strain on the country's water and sanitation infrastructure.

High amounts of water are also required for agricultural and industrial use. This comes at a time when water levels are falling across the country, and when major bodies of water are becoming increasingly polluted. Less consistent rainfall, a result of climate change, has led to droughts and the recession of major bodies of water, including Lake Victoria. Additional investments have been required to extend the water output supplying the cities of Kampala, Entebbe, and Jinja as a result. The ecological health of Lake Victoria has also been affected by pollution. The industrial sector is a major source of such pollution, resulting from the discharge of untreated or partially treated industrial waste into nearby bodies of water. Pollution is also caused by the rapidly growing urban population and the booming fish-export industry.

WASTEWATER TREATMENT AND WETLANDS

The National Water and Sewerage Corporation (NWSC) operates two conventional sewage treatment plants, in Kampala and in Masaka, which carry out primary and secondary treatment. If the quality of the treated sewage waste complies with the national environmental standards, it is then discharged either into an artificial wetland or directly into the environment. Wetlands contribute substantially to wastewater treatment. For example, the Nakivubo wetland in Kampala is estimated to contribute about $1.7 million per year to the Ugandan economy, serving as a tertiary wastewater treatment plant.

Many parts of Uganda lack access to clean water, forcing residents to collect it from local community wells, like these boys are doing here.

Water pollution poses a major health risk to the Ugandan people and underscores the need for improvements to the country's sanitation infrastructure. Areas of contaminated water act as breeding grounds for pathogens and malaria-carrying mosquitoes. When excessive rains cause flooding, this contaminated water can often end up in people's homes, causing potentially fatal disease outbreaks. Poor sanitation also leads to diarrheal diseases, which are responsible for 17 percent of all deaths of children under the age of five. It is thought that access to clean water and proper sanitation could prevent up to three-quarters of all visits to health clinics in certain parts of the country. Twenty-nine million people lack access to improved sanitation facilities, about 75 percent of the population. While the problem is worse in rural areas, Ugandans living in the slums outside of the major cities are exposed to piles of uncollected refuse on the streets, which also attract disease-carrying insects and rodents. The sanitation sector has made improvements in both areas of coverage and operational and commercial performance in the twenty-first century, but there is still work to be done. The United States Agency for International Development (USAID) recently launched a $30 million initiative to introduce water, sanitation, and hygiene interventions at the community and household levels in Uganda. These interventions are meant to increase access to clean water and proper sanitation, and to improve personal hygiene habits.

RECYCLING EFFORTS

Like most other developing societies, Uganda faces an immense challenge from excessive waste. This is especially problematic in urban areas, where the haphazard dumping of waste is prevalent. International organizations have worked with the Ugandan people to set up community-based sustainable plastic collection businesses, establish partnerships between local communities and plastic recycling companies, and promote biodegradable plastics.

One particular area of focus for these efforts was the plastic bag. Plastic bags can take up to one thousand years to break down in the environment. Once discarded, plastic bags are blown in the wind, washed into drains and watercourses, and eventually ground into the earth. Uganda is blessed with some of the richest soil in Africa, but around the towns and villages it is laced with plastic. In these areas, the layer of plastic and contaminated soil has formed an impenetrable crust that stops rain from soaking through. This leaves water stagnating in pools gurgling with methane gas bubbles.

The lack of regular sanitation services across all of Uganda leads to the accumulation of refuse in the streets, which in turn attracts scavengers like this stork.

Beginning in 1996, water hyacinth growth began to create a serious environmental and economic problem on Lake Victoria. By some estimates, the hyacinths covered up to 14,826 acres (6,000 ha) of water. When the masses of hyacinths drifted into Uganda's ports and coves, they hid fish under a vegetative screen and prevented small boats from being launched, both of which negatively impacted fishing.

The weed invasion has also been known to affect cargo boats and ferry transportation, by fouling engines and propellers and making docking difficult. Though management techniques have been initiated to deal with the plant, its infestation is unlikely to be permanently reversed.

In Uganda's capital, Kampala, discarded plastic has combined with toxic waste-management practices to make the problem worse. Although Kampala has thirty companies dealing in solid waste management, the process is mired in corruption. Poor areas of the city receive no service because it is more profitable for the companies to target wealthy areas for the user fees they collect to remove rubbish. Scavengers in the municipal dump of Kampala earn 50 Ugandan pence a day collecting plastic bags. Most plastic bags do not make it to the dump, however. In the absence of running water and proper sanitation in the city's slums, many people are forced to use the bags as toilets. These "flying latrines" (so-called because once they are filled they are typically thrown as far away as possible) are breeding grounds for disease.

To combat this problem, the government banned the manufacture, import, and use of plastic bags thinner than 0.001 inches (30 microns) in 2008; all other polythene was subject to a heavy tax. The government suggested the use of local materials, such as banana-fiber bags and papyrus baskets, as alternatives to plastic bags. At the urging of business leaders, who claimed the law disadvantaged shoppers and reduced jobs, the ban was suspended in 2015. It was reinstated in 2018, however, with the National Environmental Management Authority saying, "The economic, health, and social costs of the continued use of polythene bags outweigh the economic benefits derived from the production of bags." Efforts are also being made to improve sanitation access in the poorest parts of Uganda's cities, though millions of people still live in homes without toilets and will likely continue to scavenge for old, discarded bags.

While just one step, the ban on the plastic bag puts Uganda ahead of most of its African neighbors, and it is representative of the seriousness with which the country takes environmental issues. Though more will have to be done in the future, the country has taken meaningful steps toward combating climate change, curbing deforestation, and preserving its environment for future generations.

INTERNET LINKS

https://www.newvision.co.ug/new_vision/news/1313667/ recycling-business-ease-city-plastic-waste
This article profiles the recycling efforts of one enterprising Ugandan citizen and also contains background information on the state of sanitation and refuse collection in the country.

https://ugandacf.org
The Uganda Conservation Foundation (UCF) is a nonprofit organization established to protect Uganda's national parks and other protected areas. Its website provides information about the work it does in Uganda conserving wildlife and preserving the parks themselves.

UGANDANS

The Ugandan people come from a wide variety
of ethnic and tribal backgrounds.

6

WHEN THE BRITISH ESTABLISHED the protectorate of Uganda, they brought several ancient kingdoms and smaller societies together within the same borders. As a result, Uganda is now home to more than forty million people from a variety of ethnic and cultural backgrounds. The Bantu peoples are the most numerous, living mostly in the south of the country. In the north are found Ugandans of Nilotic and Sudanic descent. Uganda is also home to the Batwa people, a small tribe native to the slopes of the Virunga Mountains. Together, these peoples and cultures have combined to create the modern nation of Uganda.

"Let us all our people reject any idea that there is a tribe in Uganda which is more important than other tribes."
—Milton Obote

THE BANTU PEOPLES

By far the largest ethnic group in Uganda is the Bantu, who live primarily in southern Uganda. Originally hunters and gatherers, the Bantu were the first group to migrate to what is now Uganda from Central Africa. They are believed to have introduced agriculture to the region with crops

These numbers list Uganda's ethnic groups as a percentage of the total population.

Baganda . . . . 16.5 percent	Lango . . . . . . 6.3 percent
Banyankole . . . 9.6 percent	Bagisu . . . . . . 4.9 percent
Basoga . . . . . 8.8 percent	Acholi . . . . . . 4.4 percent
Bakiga . . . . . . 7.1 percent	Lugbara . . . . . 3.3 percent
Iteso . . . . 7.0 percent	Other . . . . . . 32.1 percent

The Baganda have long been the largest single ethnic group in Uganda and were historically the rulers of the kingdom of Buganda.

such as millet and sorghum. Although they split into many tribal groups and developed multiple languages, the Bantu tribes share one important characteristic that makes them easily identifiable: the names of most of the Bantu tribal groups begin with the prefix "Ba-." The largest of the Bantu tribes is the Baganda. Other Bantu peoples include the Basoga, Bagwe, Bagisu, Banyankole, Basamia, and the Kenyi.

The largest of the traditional kingdoms in modern-day Uganda is Buganda, which was historically the kingdom of the Baganda people. Though the Baganda were willing to recognize talent in whoever displayed it, their society was still one with a strict hierarchy. The lowest social stratum was a class of people known as the *bakopi* (BA-koh-pee), or serfs, who owed their livelihood to the goodwill of the *baami* (BAA-mee), or chiefs, and the *balangira* (BA-lan-gee-ra), or princes. The *baami* were, in effect, the middle class in Baganda society. This status was not strictly hereditary and could be obtained through distinguished service, ability, or royal appointment. The highest class was the *balangira*, the aristocracy who based their right to rule on royal blood. At the very top of this class was the kabaka, or king. Kabakas valued both their male heirs and their female family members. The queen mother was given the title *namasole* (NA-ma-so-lay), while royal sisters were referred to as *nalinya* (NA-leen-ya).

As a result of the concentration of power in the south of the protectorate during the colonial era, the Bantu peoples were favored by the British government and received more education and economic opportunities. The

Traditional Baganda attire consists of a bark cloth (pictured) wrapped from the chest to the feet and tied around the waist with a thick belt. Called a kanzu *(KAN-zoo), the garment is partly covered by another piece of bark cloth tied around the shoulders. Bark cloth is made from the inner layer of a tree's bark, a material that becomes more resistant and supple the more it is dampened and beaten. Arab traders introduced* kanzus *to the country. Today, many* kanzus *are made of cotton or linen. As the formal attire for all Baganda men, the* kanzu *is worn with a suit jacket or a sport coat.*

legacy of this favoritism can still be seen today, as Ugandans of Bantu descent hold a disproportionate share of academic, religious, and governmental positions.

THE NILOTIC AND SUDANIC PEOPLES

The Nilotic peoples can be divided into two subgroups: the Nilo-Hamitic and the Luo. Both groups are found in northern and eastern Uganda. Also referred to as the Lango, the Nilo-Hamitic can trace their origins to Ethiopia and are mainly pastoralists.

Ugandans descended from the Acholi tribe are traditionally found in the north of the country.

The Luo peoples, which include the Acholi, the Alur, the Jonam, and the Japadhola tribes, migrated from southern Sudan. They live in western, northern, and eastern Uganda. The Acholi tribe was traditionally organized in chiefdoms, each under a hereditary ruler known as the *rwot*. The *rwot* was a link between the living and the dead and offered sacrifices to ancestors on behalf of the people. The administrative structures of the Luo were similar to the precolonial kingdoms of Buganda, Bunyoro, Ankole, and Toro.

The Sudanic tribes of the West Nile originated in Sudan, but over the generations their culture and language became distinct from those of present-day Sudan. About 6 percent of Ugandans—the Lugbara, the Madi, and a few small groups in the northwestern corner of the country—speak Central Sudanic

Roughly fifteen thousand Ugandans of Sudanese descent are classified as Nubians, in reference to their ancestral origin near the Nuba Mountains in Sudan. They are descendants of Sudanese military recruits who entered Uganda in the late nineteenth century as part of the colonial army employed to quell popular revolts. Since the fall of Idi Amin, who favored the Nubian population because of their religious and military background, these Ugandans have become dispersed across major urban areas. The largest concentration of Nubians is in the Bombo district. Nubians are mostly Muslim, and while some still speak Sudanese Arabic, the younger generations primarily speak Kinubi, a language that mixes Arabic and Luganda.

languages. During the colonial era, the Lugbara language was encouraged in elementary schools, allowing the Lugbara people to dominate their neighbors.

THE BATWA PEOPLE

The Batwa people of the Virunga Mountains have struggled to adapt to life in Uganda since being removed from their ancestral homelands.

By far the most marginalized group in Uganda is the Batwa people. Native to the Virunga Mountains along the southwestern border with the Democratic Republic of the Congo, the Batwa are a pygmy people, whose adult men grow to less than 5 feet (1.5 m) tall. Originally hunter-gatherers, the Batwa people survived off the natural bounty of the forests, living in huts made of leaves and branches and deriving medicine from herbs. Anthropologists estimate that tribes like the Batwa have lived in Africa's forests for over sixty thousand years.

This centuries-old way of life was permanently changed, however, when the Bwindi Impenetrable Forest was made a national park and a World Heritage Site in 1991. Humans were forbidden from living permanently within the forest, and the Batwa were forcibly evicted from their homes by the Uganda Wildlife Authority (UWA). The Batwa were not given any compensation for losing their homeland, as Ugandan authorities claimed they never legally owned it in the first place. This reduced the Batwa to landless squatters, with no homes and no futures. The skills learned over generations in the forest were not transferable to the modern world, and without access to the shelter and herbal remedies provided by the trees, the Batwa began dying younger. The average Batwa person now lives on less than seventy-five cents a day, and their nomadic lifestyle prevents their children from going to school. Racist writings and stereotypical images of the Batwa have convinced many Ugandans that they are uncivilized or subhuman peoples, which contributes to their ongoing marginalization and exclusion from mainstream society. A 2002 population census determined that there were six thousand Batwa people living in southwest Uganda; that number is likely lower in 2018.

As a final humiliation, some of the only work available to members of the Batwa tribe is as guides along the Batwa Cultural Trail, a tourist attraction established by the UWA. The tours involve treks into the forests where the Batwa once lived, in which the members of the tribe reenact scenes from their former lives for tourists. This grotesque pantomime would not have been out of place in a nineteenth-century freak show, with the pain and loss of the Batwa exploited for money. Though the UWA claims that half of the revenue generated from the trail is returned to the Batwa, the tribe insists they have not seen any of this money. The Batwa have been unable to gain even the most basic recognition of their human rights, and they have no ability to meaningfully participate in Uganda's political life. While the other peoples of Uganda have slowly managed to develop a sense of understanding and respect for one another, the marginalization of the Batwa remains a glaring example of discrimination and oppression, and one in dire need of reparation.

> "The hope is to be given land of our own. That would be peace. Even if our children had no access to the forest, they could have a future."
> —Stephen, a tour guide on the Batwa Cultural Trail

INTERNET LINKS

https://www.everyculture.com/wc/Tajikistan-to-Zimbabwe/Baganda.html
The Baganda people are profiled in-depth here, with information provided about their cultural heritage, family life, language, and folklore.

http://ugandatourismcenter.com/place/batwa-people-and-their-culture
This link provides further information on the Batwa people and their culture, as well as a brief overview of the historical basis for the discrimination and prejudice faced by the tribe today.

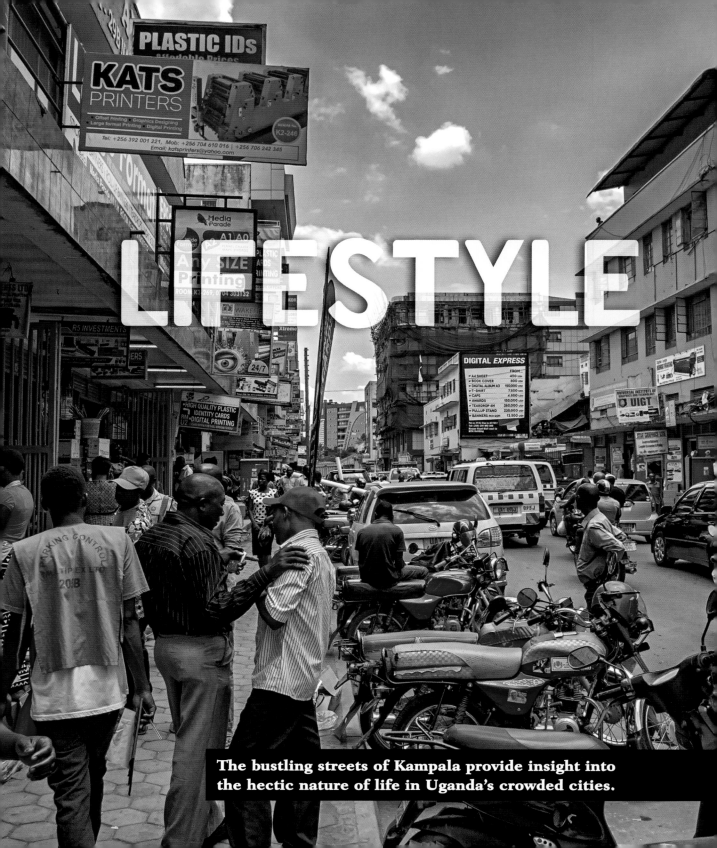

LIFESTYLE

The bustling streets of Kampala provide insight into the hectic nature of life in Uganda's crowded cities.

7

LIFE IN UGANDA IS FILLED WITH challenges, some unique to particular groups of people and some that cut across all strata of society. Urban Ugandans live a Westernized life and encounter problems common to cities across the developing world. In the countryside, many rural communities maintain some semblance of their traditional lifestyles, adhering to older notions of proper familial arrangements and gender roles. Women and LGBT individuals face unique and often extreme discrimination as a result of these attitudes. Whether urban or rural, almost all Ugandans face difficulties in receiving adequate health care and education. Life is hard for the Ugandan people, and it is a challenge for many just to survive.

"It is better that trials come to you in the beginning and you find peace afterwards than that they come to you at the end."
—Ugandan proverb

PHONES AND THE INTERNET

Internet and phone access in Uganda have improved dramatically in recent years. Though very few Ugandans have a landline, 63 percent of the population uses mobile devices. Virtually every region of the country now has phone service. Internet access has also become vastly more affordable and accessible. There are eighteen million internet users in the country, the majority of whom access the internet through their mobile devices; this number is growing yearly. Social media sites are popular in Uganda, with Facebook the most commonly used.

CITY LIFE

Although Ugandans are becoming more similar through the influence of modern communications technology and increasing intermarriage between tribal groups, most Ugandans' lifestyles are still largely determined by where they live. For city dwellers, this means a mostly atomized, individual existence, a marked contrast from the traditional villages, where entire generations of a family live in either the same house or within walking distance of one another. Uganda's population is incredibly young (nearly 70 percent of the population is under the age of twenty-four) and expanding rapidly, meaning young people migrate to the cities by the thousands looking for work. This has led to crowded living conditions and put strains on urban infrastructure, with roads and sanitation systems experiencing regular breakdowns. Electricity is inconsistent in even the largest urban areas, and the cost of living is often higher than many Ugandans can afford. Some young men and women who come to the cities lack the education or specialized training needed to take high-paying jobs, and without a support system to fall back on, they are forced to turn to crime or prostitution to survive. Slums exist outside of most major cities, alongside middle-class suburbs, highlighting the wealth inequality that exists in Uganda. Often, the path to steady employment is marked by bribery or simply by knowing the right person. For young women, sexual exploitation and/or assault are additional worries when interacting not only with potential employers but also landlords or police. Women of all ages are also forced to juggle work with domestic duties, as Ugandan men are often not home to help with children and household duties. While some Ugandans are able to make a comfortable life for themselves in the cities, most residents struggle to survive on just a few dollars a day. This disparity in economic outcomes, combined with President Museveni's attempts to cling to power, has fueled dissatisfaction among the Ugandan youth, who feel their country is indifferent to their futures. Many are desperate to see some kind of change to the status quo.

These homes in eastern Uganda, with their mud walls and grass-thatched roofs, illustrate the country's traditional rural architecture.

RURAL LIFE

Despite the growth of the cities, Uganda's population is still overwhelmingly rural. Among agricultural peoples, the traditional residential pattern was one of scattered homesteads, each surrounded by its own arable land and some reserved pastureland. This way of life is still very much in evidence in rural parts of Uganda today. Round houses with wooden frames, mud walls, and grass-thatched, conical roofs are common throughout agricultural regions. In the past, rural economies were all essentially subsistence-based—each household raised its own food supply and made its own clothes and houses. Specialization, other than ironworking, was unusual, and government consisted of one man selected from the village to settle disputes and interact with local tribal chiefs. In modern Uganda, the villages are incorporated into the national economy, allowing farmers to sell their produce in larger markets. Rural areas are also represented in the country's Parliament, though tribal leadership persists in certain regions. The traditional kingdoms of the south are still given some autonomy in internal affairs, and smaller tribes throughout the country maintain many of their traditions, particularly regarding social arrangements.

In the past in rural areas, each household was traditionally ruled by a male head, who lived with his wife (or wives), his married sons (and their wives and children), and sometimes his younger brothers, all within a single, fenced enclosure. Even when a man had only one wife, he often had an additional separate room or house where he kept his possessions and entertained visitors. It was thought to be the moral and economic responsibility of the family head to ensure the production of sufficient food for his household. The men cleared the bush, built the homes, and bartered with one another, while the women tilled the land.

The women and children of the house were the traditional nucleus of the family and the center of domestic activity. Each wife had her own house, sometimes partly or wholly fenced off, or at least her own room in the large house. A wife usually also had her own kitchen hearth, where she cooked for the family, and she often also had her own food store or granary. Women were responsible not only for food preparation but also for household management, child-rearing, care of the sick and elderly, and overall family health and welfare. Rural boys were taught skills by their fathers, among them herding, fighting, hunting, and agriculture. Girls were instructed by their mothers in the proper ways of cooking, basketry, pottery, childcare, and other functions related to managing the household. In some tribes, both boys and girls underwent circumcision as a rite of passage.

In rural areas today, life remains difficult. While polygamy is rarely practiced and most families no longer have a formal head, the daily struggles faced by rural Ugandans are much the same. Most rural dwellings continue to be mud huts with dirt floors, and days are occupied from dawn to dusk with basic household chores. Men and women work to raise crops and often walk miles to collect clean water. Women continue to be responsible for managing the household, preparing meals, and doing the family's laundry. Many rural children are forced to help their parents with their farms and are kept out of school either due to necessity or because their parents cannot afford to pay for books and uniforms. While some of the specific tasks or duties performed by men and women have fallen out of practice among most rural Ugandans, the broader gender roles assigned by tradition have persisted. Men and women who defy gender expectations face ostracism from their communities or worse. These conservative views have had a disproportionately negative impact on Ugandan women, girls, and LGBT individuals.

IMPORTANT LIFE EVENTS

Tribal customs persist most strongly around important milestones in the lives of Ugandan citizens. Birth, marriage, and death are all characterized by a variety of rituals and beliefs, and the second-class status of women in much of Ugandan society is derived from these traditions.

BIRTH   Uganda has a very high fertility rate, at roughly five children per woman. It has a maternal mortality rate of 343 maternal deaths for every 100,000 births. This is largely due to the lack of proper care given to women during labor. Most rural women give birth at home rather than in a hospital, and only 58 percent of births are attended by a skilled health professional. The youth of so many mothers is also a factor; a Ugandan survey conducted in 2016 found that 19 percent of girls between the ages of fifteen and nineteen already had at least one child, and another 5 percent were pregnant with their first. On an individual level, however, women have a relatively low chance of dying from maternal causes. International organization UNICEF reports that Ugandan women have a 2 percent lifetime risk of maternal death.

Many Ugandan women become mothers at a very young age, and not all are able to access the health care necessary during their pregnancies.

Traditional views of women are largely responsible for the youth of so many first-time mothers. In the past, women were expected to marry and have children very young, as that was perceived to be their primary role in tribal society. Historically, as soon as a Ugandan woman was married she was expected to conceive a child. If this did not happen, questions would be asked, and if it took longer than a year or so to produce a baby, the husband was at liberty to marry another woman.

Among the tribes today, families with the most children are still accorded the most respect, and a woman with many children is considered better than a woman with few or none. Boys are also thought to be more valuable than girls. This notion starts the dismissal of women as equals to men from the beginning, in the cradle.

In cities, where these attitudes are less prevalent, young women find themselves more vulnerable to economic pressures. Since many lack an education and therefore struggle to find well-paying work, they are often forced to attach themselves to men with some money, an arrangement that commonly leads to a pregnancy. Women employed in formal jobs are given twelve weeks

Though some newborns in Ugandan tribal communities are named immediately after birth, others remain nameless until they begin to continuously cry. The naming of the child might also wait until the umbilical cord falls off, at which time the names are given by the grandmother or aunt of the baby. Other infants do not receive a name until the third day after their birth, when they are named by the woman who helped in the delivery. Some traditions claim that an ancestor appears in a dream and dictates a name for the child. These names can reflect the circumstances under which the child was born, echo the name of a relative, or simply be the day of the week or place of the infant's birth.

of paid maternity leave, but since the vast majority of Ugandan women work on either farms or in informal positions, this benefit is not widely distributed.

There are many customs associated with birth among tribal communities. After the child is born, the placenta is often buried, and the woman is confined to the home for a number of days. Sometimes she cannot even accept food from a member of her husband's clan until her days of confinement are over, although this practice is rare today. A variation of this custom involves confining a woman to the house until the umbilical cord has broken from her child's navel. The cords are sometimes preserved in a special gourd, and the mother keeps the cords from all of her children. In some tribes, women are also not allowed to look at the sky before the umbilical cord breaks off.

MARRIAGE   For all Ugandans, marriage is a very important part of life. Among some Baganda, women are not respected by the tribe until they are married, nor is a man regarded as being complete until he has a wife. Rural communities of all tribes are heavily invested in heterosexual marriages, and anyone that does not partake in one faces social shaming or worse.

In previous eras, parents would initiate and conduct marriage arrangements for their children. Before the marriage, an important clan ceremony, *okwanjula* (ok-wan-JOO-la), would be held. In this ceremony, the husband-to-be, escorted by his relatives and friends, would visit the relatives of the bride to introduce his clan to them. Girls were required to be virgins at the time of their marriage, and having children before getting married was looked down upon. In the event of a divorce, which was common in Buganda, a portion of any dowry given to the husband would be repaid. The amount returned depended on the length of the marriage and whether the woman had given birth to any children. Among some rural tribes, arranged marriages are still carried out. Families often choose their children's spouses early in life, usually without any consent or input from the affianced.

Drums and dancing are both integral parts of traditional tribal wedding ceremonies in Uganda.

DEATH There have always been a great number of superstitions attached to death among Ugandan tribes. Traditionally, burials took place after five days, after which there was a further month of mourning. Ten days after this period there would be funeral rites known as *okwabya olumbe* (ok-wa-by-YA o-LOOM-bay), an important ceremony to which all clan elders and relatives were invited. The ceremony included eating, drinking, dancing, and the installation of an heir, who would take on the responsibilities of the deceased if he had been a man and the head of a family. Other events would also take place at the ceremony, such as *okwalula abaana* (ok-wa-loo-LA ah-BA-na), in which children would be formally identified as belonging to the clan and given clan names (this is why many Baganda have more than two names).

Other tribes treated death in more unique ways. Among the Bagwe, if someone died everyone was expected to weep loudly; anyone who did not would be suspected of having caused the death. When anyone died in the Japadhola culture, the corpse would remain overnight in the house in the exact spot where it had been found. Everyone who lived in the house camped outside, and none of them were allowed to bathe for at least three days.

Many of these traditions persist today among Uganda's tribes. For some rural populations, the hiring of professional mourners has been a unique modern addition to traditional funeral rites. For a set fee, mourners will show up to a funeral and cry loudly and fiercely. This practice has grown in popularity among some rural Ugandans because of traditions that state that loud wailing at a funeral is a sign of love for the deceased; the louder the cries, the more loved was the deceased. In the cities, funeral homes carry out ceremonies similar to those in the United States or Europe. Different funeral homes offer a variety of services, ranging from simply collecting the remains of a loved one and transporting them to the cemetery, to planning and carrying out a church ceremony and outfitting the family of the deceased with elegant outfits.

LGBT RIGHTS

The emphasis on traditional family structures and the importance attached to motherhood in Uganda not only limit opportunities for women but also have profound implications for the country's LGBT population. Uganda is one of thirty-six countries in Africa (and one of more than seventy worldwide) where homosexuality is illegal. "Carnal knowledge of any person against the order of nature" is prohibited by law, and the Uganda Anti-Homosexuality Act, signed in 2014 but later annulled, made it legal to imprison people for life for "aggravated homosexuality." This was actually a softening of the bill's original language, which called for the death penalty for homosexuals. Though this particular law has been deemed invalid by the Constitutional Court of Uganda, the climate of fear and discrimination produced by it has been long-lasting.

While anti-sodomy laws have been on the books in Uganda since the colonial period, they largely went unenforced. Frank Mugisha, the leader of the LGBT advocacy group Sexual Minorities Uganda (SMUG), as well as other local activists, has pointed to the influence of Christian fundamentalists from the United States in making homosexuality into a major issue in the late 2000s. Figures like Tony Perkins of the Family Research Council and Scott Lively began getting involved in African politics throughout that decade, always pushing for extremely right-wing, fundamentalist Christian laws, particularly regarding homosexuality. Both men were involved in the drafting of the Anti-Homosexuality Act and have given talks throughout the country supporting its passage. Warning of the "evil institution" of homosexuality and its goal of defeating "the marriage-based society," Lively and others like him have found a receptive audience in Ugandans from socially conservative backgrounds with strict gender norms. Many Ugandans feel that homosexuality is a Western import and not native to Uganda, making members of the LGBT community inherently untrustworthy. The rhetoric of the antigay preachers also preys on the fears of parents, as they falsely claim that exposure to homosexuality can "corrupt" children. It is all nonsense, but it has caught on with many Ugandans, including some in the government. Ethics Minister Simon Lokodo is one of the leading antigay voices in Museveni's administration; he uses disgusting terminology to refer to gay men and women, and pushes abusive conversion therapy programs in the country.

This 2015 Pride celebration was one of the last to take place in Uganda without police interference. The country's LGBT community faces harsh discrimination from both the state and private individuals.

The violence and intimidation faced by the LGBT community in this climate comes from both the police and government officials, as well as from private individuals. Pride events have been brutally suppressed for the past several years, with police arresting activists and beating participants. SMUG documented 264 cases of human rights abuses targeted at LGBT individuals between May 2014 and December 2015, forty-eight of which involved violence, including "torture by the state." Eleven physical attacks were reported against members of the LGBT community in early 2017 alone, including one in which a person was doused with gasoline and lit on fire by a mob. Gay teenagers find themselves in an especially dire situation, as they risk expulsion from their communities if their sexual orientation is discovered. In the most extreme circumstances, gay people are either beaten to death by their communities or subjected to rapes designed to "correct" their sexuality. More common are the everyday forms of discrimination, in which known or suspected homosexuals are denied employment, housing, or education. Hundreds of LGBT Ugandans have fled the country and sought asylum in Kenya, where anti-homosexuality laws are less strictly enforced.

Despite these many obstacles, Mugisha and other activists continue pushing for equality. They believe that as the gay community becomes more visible, it will gain greater support from Ugandans, who will realize that homosexuality is a normal part of life and not foreign to the country. Activists also point to the international condemnation that the Anti-Homosexuality Act received, as well as the decreasing prominence of antigay pastors as reasons for optimism; Scott Lively was sued by SMUG for violating international law in his efforts to persecute Uganda's gay community, though the case was eventually dismissed in 2017. Homosexuality remains against the law in Uganda—legally, nothing has changed. Activists working to change that law, however, believe that the political climate is turning in their favor. Young people are largely supportive of the LGBT community, and there are friendly venues at which Pride events can quietly be held. With continued activism and pressure, it is hoped that Uganda's LGBT community can realize equal treatment under the law in the near future.

HEALTH CARE

Though health services in Uganda are theoretically available to all, in reality only half of the population has access to medical facilities. There are more than one hundred hospitals in the country, but 80 percent are located in urban areas. Rural Ugandans are often forced to rely instead on small clinics or local medical practitioners. Despite this disparity, health outcomes are improving in Uganda. There is roughly one doctor for every ten thousand Ugandans, the best ratio the country has seen since the departure of most health care professionals under the Amin regime. Life expectancy stands at fifty-five years for men and fifty-eight years for women as of 2017. Efforts to improve access to health care have been made, but the fact that public health expenditures only account for 7.2 percent of Uganda's GDP limits how effective these efforts can be. Other challenges include disease prevention, a lack of reproductive health, and HIV/AIDS persistence.

There remains a high risk of infectious disease in Uganda, partially due to the lack of clean water in the country. Malaria, bacterial diarrhea, hepatitis A and E, typhoid fever, measles, and African sleeping sickness are some of the most prevalent. These diseases have their greatest effects on the very young and the very old. Uganda's older population, which will increase sharply once the country's overwhelmingly young citizens begin aging, have trouble accessing health-care services, both due to poverty and physical disabilities. Those with money, family, and means of transportation are able to get the treatments they need, but poor older Ugandans are often discouraged from seeking care by the long travel distances and unavailability of needed medication.

The lack of proper reproductive health care poses a major problem for Ugandan women. In 2013, 52 percent of all pregnancies were unplanned, and about one-quarter of them were terminated, demonstrating the massive, unmet need for contraception in Uganda. Only 30 percent of married women and 52 percent of unmarried women use contraceptives regularly, and abortion is illegal except in cases of rape, incest, or if the mother's life is in danger. Even these abortions are incredibly hard to access, however, forcing most women to undergo unsafe and potentially deadly abortions outside of designated health facilities.

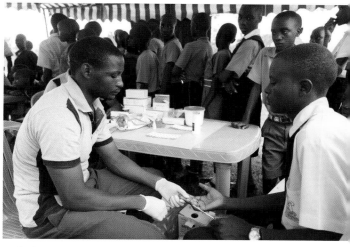

Health clinics in Uganda provide much-needed services to rural Ugandans and carry out tests for HIV.

The influence of evangelical Christians on the government has led to banning sexual education in Uganda's schools, and government funds are not spent on reproductive health services. International nonprofit organizations have stepped in to fill this void, offering free contraception to Ugandan men and women, as well as education about healthy sexual behavior. Myths about contraception causing cancer have been dispelled, contraceptive use has improved, and maternal mortality rates (and abortion rates) have decreased as a result. These programs have recently been jeopardized, however, by the reinstatement by the Trump administration of the "global gag rule," which prevents American money from going to any international organizations that provide abortions, suggest them as a viable family planning method, or lobby to make the procedure legal in countries where it is banned. This has had a major impact on family planning groups in Uganda, who will lose tens of millions of dollars in funding as a result of the rule. Their activities will likely be scaled back, and Ugandan women, especially those in poor, rural areas, will lose access to much-needed health services. Unplanned pregnancies, and therefore unsafe abortions, will also almost certainly increase.

These HIV-positive Ugandans are rehearsing a play that they use to educate their fellow citizens about the transmission of the virus as well as the treatments available.

Uganda was also hit very hard by the HIV/AIDS epidemic that began in the 1980s, and it remains one of the leading causes of death in the country, claiming the lives of twenty-six thousand people in 2017 alone. About 1.3 million people are living with HIV in Uganda today, with men more affected than women (14.3 percent of men, compared with 8.8 percent of women).

Stigma against vulnerable populations, as well as against HIV-positive individuals, has been a major barrier in treating the disease. More than half of all HIV-positive Ugandans report having been subject to gossip or verbal harassment for their status, and are also denied employment in some cases. This has led many Ugandans to fear getting tested, or to refuse to share the results of their tests with their sexual partners, furthering the spread of the disease. Punitive laws targeting gay men, sex workers, and people who inject drugs have also prevented treatment from reaching the populations that most need it.

Despite these challenges, treatment has proved effective in Uganda. An educational campaign was launched in the 1990s to inform the public about the disease and how it is spread, which resulted in a decrease in the rate of infection, the first such improvement in all of sub-Saharan Africa. Efforts continue to this day to educate the populace and encourage testing, to ensure that everyone knows his or her status. The number of people getting tested doubled between 2012 and 2015, with women getting tested at higher rates than men. In total, an estimated 81 percent of people living with HIV are aware of their status, a number that shows the progress that has been made as well as how much work still needs to be done. Condom distribution has also been successful but could go even further.

As of 2016, more than 1,700 health facilities across the country were offering antiretroviral treatment (ART) to nearly nine hundred thousand people. There are still HIV-positive individuals going untested and untreated, however, meaning these efforts are not addressing the entirety of the problem. Material

FEMALE GENITAL MUTILATION

Female genital mutilation (FGM), also known as female circumcision, is a barbaric practice carried out by some tribes in Uganda. FGM, usually performed on girls as a rite of passage into adulthood, involves the partial or total removal of the external genitalia. Those subjected to it can suffer potentially life-threatening infections or face serious complications later in life when having sex or giving birth. The procedure does permanent physical and psychological damage, and has been performed on approximately two hundred million girls and women worldwide. In Uganda, FGM was formally outlawed in 2010, with lengthy jail sentences imposed on anyone caught carrying out the procedure. While this has greatly reduced the prevalence of FGM in Uganda, it has not wiped it out entirely. Though only 1.4 percent of women nationwide have undergone the procedure, that number rises to as high as 95 percent among the tribes where it is still a regular part of life. In these tribes, women that refuse to undergo the procedure are ostracized from the community and denied the opportunity to get married. Since the procedure is now illegal, it is carried out in secret, with many tribal members crossing the border into Kenya to perform the operation. Some survivors of FGM have banded together to spread awareness of the practice and encourage its end, teaching young girls to stay in school and shun the procedure if it is urged on them. Though it is difficult to get this message to some of the communities that most need it, activists agree that keeping girls in school, where they can be educated about the dangers of the procedure, is likely the best way to deal with the problem.

and human resources are strained, with clinics running out of testing kits and not having enough staff on hand to carry out the tests or the treatments. The government is also reliant on outside donors to make up a significant portion of the funds dedicated to fighting the disease, a precarious situation that could implode at the whim of any of those donors. With new infections expected to rise rapidly over the course of the next decade, the government needs to increase its funding to the public health sector to keep the disease under control. It also needs to abandon its laws targeting homosexuals and drug users, to ensure that these populations can receive the treatment that they need.

THE EDUCATION SYSTEM

Education in Uganda is greatly hampered by poverty, and few students make it all the way through secondary school. Sixty-five percent of students drop out of primary school, and only 31 percent of Ugandans over the age of twenty-five have some secondary education. Girls are more likely to drop out of school than boys, most commonly due to pregnancy or to get married. This has led to a higher rate of illiteracy among girls and women than among men; overall, the literacy rate in the country stands at 78 percent, though among women it is only 71 percent. Education only accounts for 2.3 percent of GDP spending, an indication of the low priority placed on it by the government.

Formal education in Uganda was first started by missionary organizations in the late nineteenth century. The local government took control in the 1920s and began expanding access throughout the 1950s and 1960s. The reign of Amin interrupted educational progress, as many schools were neglected or closed. The education system was rebuilt in the 1980s and 1990s, and it now consists of seven years of primary school, beginning at age six, and six years of secondary school, beginning at age thirteen. Children are only legally required to attend

Children in Uganda face serious challenges in receiving an education, and many are forced to drop out of school to help earn money for their families.

HIGHER EDUCATION

There are a number of colleges and universities in Uganda, including teacher training colleges and technical schools. The most well-known is Makerere University in Kampala (shown here). Started as a technical school in 1922, it was the first major institution of higher learning in all of East and Central Africa. Still operating today, Makerere University has become a very good school, attracting students from across Africa.

The Islamic University in Uganda (IUIU) is located in the city of Mbale. Since its opening in 1988, IUIU has steadily increased the size of its student body. It currently boasts seventy-two academic programs taught by faculty from eight different countries.

The Ugandan government gives out about four thousand university scholarships per year, though many students interested in pursuing postsecondary education opt to study abroad.

through primary school, but many do not even make it that far. Though the government provides for free education at all public primary schools, as well as for secondary students who do well enough on their final primary school exams, the cost of books, supplies, and uniforms is often more than students and their families can bear. Many students are forced to drop out when they can no longer afford these costs, or simply because they need to help their parents put food on the table.

Class sizes are very large, with an average of forty-three pupils per teacher in primary schools. Teachers themselves are often poorly trained, and many are so poorly paid that they are forced to take second jobs to make ends meet, limiting the amount of time they have to prepare lessons and work with students. Some students also face physical and sexual abuse from their teachers and classmates.

Education outcomes also vary between different geographic areas of Uganda. Parts of the northern regions of the country are still recovering from the dislocation and destruction inflicted by the Lord's Resistance Army (LRA), which resulted in millions of Ugandans fleeing their homelands and the closure of dozens of schools. In these areas, the poverty rate is as high as 49 percent, preventing many children from being able to afford school uniforms and books. Many of the adults there also have low levels of literacy and are therefore unable to help their children with schoolwork. Finding qualified teachers is another challenge, particularly among women. Only 12 percent of teachers in these regions are women, which discourages female students from seeing a future for themselves in education. School performance is even worse in some rural, eastern communities, where lack of proper funding for educational materials has driven many children to seek a living in the fields or on the streets.

In an effort to improve education outcomes, the Ugandan government allowed Bridge International Academies (BIA), a private educational company, to open sixty-three schools in the country in 2015. Founded in Kenya in 2007 by American entrepreneurs, BIA aims to provide education to underserved areas. It does this by churning out school buildings through an in-house production company and giving teachers lessons to be read word-for-word from a tablet. It also charges fees that are well outside the budgetary range of most poor citizens, especially if they want to ensure that their children receive a lunch. BIA operates schools in multiple countries and receives money from many of the world's richest people.

Despite being flush with cash, the BIA schools in Uganda have been plagued with problems, and the Ugandan government began attempting to push the company out of the country in 2016. The Bridge schools in Uganda lacked proper licensing and rushed into operation without properly training their teachers, establishing curricula, or even finishing construction. The schools received harsh criticism from education advocates, who pointed out that BIA was more interested in generating a profit than in providing a quality education. Teachers' unions were also against the push to privatize schooling, arguing that the low wages paid in these schools drove down wages for teachers everywhere.

Though BIA claimed it was offering parents a choice for their children's education, this choice only existed for parents who were able to afford the schools' fees. And while privatizing schools would only affect a small number of families in the short-term, in the long run it has the potential to create a two-tiered education system in the country.

With comparatively wealthier students leaving public schools to attend private institutions, outcomes in public schools will almost certainly worsen. This will disincentivize further investments in them and lead to more privatization, which will ultimately result in a situation where only wealthy and middle-class children are able to receive an education of any real quality. This violates the core principle of education as a public good available to all citizens, and demonstrates the need for increased government funding for the public-school system.

The Ugandan High Court ordered the closing of the BIA schools in late 2016, citing their unsanitary learning conditions, unqualified teachers, and lack of proper licensing as reasons for the decision. BIA appealed, but the court ruled against them again in 2018, stating that the company deliberately violated Ugandan laws in setting up their schools. This will hopefully serve as a wake-up call for the future. Though Uganda's public schools no doubt have serious problems, the solution to those problems is sustained public investment, not privatization. As is the case with health care, only an ongoing commitment on the part of the government to improving outcomes for its citizens, be they educational or health-related, will ensure that Ugandans can live a fulfilled life.

INTERNET LINKS

https://www.avert.org/professionals/hiv-around-world/sub-saharan-africa/uganda
The HIV/AIDS epidemic in Uganda is profiled here, with plenty of information about the populations most vulnerable to the disease, the various treatment options available, and the challenges that still remain in combating the crisis.

https://sexualminoritiesuganda.com
Sexual Minorities Uganda (SMUG) is a nonprofit advocacy organization dedicated to advancing the rights of Uganda's LGBT community. Their website provides updates on the oppression facing the country's LGBT citizens, as well as information about upcoming events.

RELIGION

Crowds of Ugandans pray and sing during a
massive Christian church service; Christianity

8

LIKE MOST OTHER ASPECTS OF LIFE IN Uganda, the country's modern religious makeup was heavily influenced by British imperialism. Most Ugandans followed traditional tribal religions in the years before the arrival of the Europeans, believing that the spirits of their ancestors and other supreme beings could influence the lives of those on Earth. The arrival of missionaries and traders in the nineteenth century changed that forever. Both Catholicism and Protestant Christianity were introduced to the region, and they remain the most dominant religions in the country today. Islam was also adopted by some Ugandans at the same time, while immigrants from South Asia developed a small Hindu community.

Today, the traditional tribal religions have largely vanished, though some tribes still maintain elements of their former faiths. The Ugandan constitution provides for freedom of religion, allowing the people to worship whatever god or gods they choose and to practice their religions freely. Though there is some tension between religious groups, the communities have lived together in peace since the end of the civil war.

TRIBAL RELIGIONS

In the years before the protectorate of Uganda was established, the tribes of the region held a variety of religious beliefs. The Baganda believed in Katonda, the supreme being who created the heavens and the earth. Katonda was also believed to be one of the superhuman spirits who took the form of a *mizimu* (mi-ZEE-moo) or a *misambwa* (mi-SAM-bwa). The *mizimu* were believed to be the ghosts of the dead, an extended existence of the soul after physical death. Such ghosts would haunt anyone the dead person held a grudge against. If the *mizimu* entered natural objects, such as stones or trees, the *mizimu* would become a *misambwa*.

Like the Baganda, the Basoga believed in a supreme being, Lubaale, as well as several other deities. Human beings were believed to work as messengers of their ancestors, Lubaale, or other gods. To the Basoga, the spirit world, places of worship, animated objects, and fetishes all had power to do good or evil to the living. The Acholi believed in a supreme being called Jok and in another god, Lubanga, who was the cause of evil and had to be appeased at all times. They also worshipped the spirits of the dead and believed that they would help the surviving members of their families if appropriate devotion was shown to their memories.

The Basamia and the Bagwe believed in a supreme being and in ancestral spirits that intervened in human affairs and caused harm, death, and misfortune if not appeased. Each family had an *indaro* (in-DA-ro), or shrine, where they would offer sacrifices to their ancestors.

The Bakonjo believed in two supreme beings, Kalisa and Nyabarika. Kalisa was half-man and half-monster. Nyabarika was believed to be the most powerful spiritual being, with the ability to heal, kill, haunt, provide fertility or cause barrenness, and make hunting expeditions successful. Since the Bakonjo regarded hunting as a very important activity, both for sport and as a source

Each tribe had its own rules, among which were specific taboos that children were taught from a young age not to violate. The taboos varied from clan to clan. In some tribes, no one would eat the flesh of the animal that was considered to be his or her lucky totem. Parents were not allowed to sleep in the same hut as their son-in-law, and once children were considered adults, they would not sleep in the same hut as their parents. Among the Bunyoro, pregnant women were not allowed to attend burials for fear that they might miscarry. Graves were also marked with stones or iron rods so that nobody would build over them. If the graves were built over, it was believed that all the surviving members of the family would fall ill and die.

of food, skilled hunters enjoyed a position of importance in their society as being divinely favored.

Worship of these gods was not a matter of routine among the tribes but was dictated by misfortunes or diseases. In the case of a misfortune, the family head would approach a special diviner known as a *julam bira* (joo-LAM bee-RA), an *iolam wara* (eye-oh-LAM wa-RA), or an *ajoga* (eye-YO-ga) to have the cause of the misfortune diagnosed.

Wearing beads and goat skin, a member of the Bagisu tribe parades through the streets as part of a traditional religious ceremony.

IMPORTED RELIGIONS

The advent of colonialism and the introduction of foreign religions in the second half of the nineteenth century transformed the traditional cultures of Uganda. With the adoption of Islam and Christianity, it became fashionable to communicate with God in Arabic, Latin, and English. The manner of worship changed greatly, as traditional shrines were replaced with mosques or churches, with seats, organs, and electricity. Prayers became regular on Fridays for Muslims and on Sundays for Christians, and were no longer dictated by particular instances of want or trouble. Organized religion gradually became a belief and a way of life.

While some Ugandans continue to mix traditional beliefs and practices with those of their adopted faiths, in many parts of the country the old religious traditions have faded into memory in favor of Christianity, Islam, or Hinduism.

CHRISTIANITY

Christianity is by far the most prominent religion in Uganda, with 84 percent of citizens identifying as belonging to one denomination or another. The arrival of the first Christian missionaries, Anglican and Catholic, took place in the kingdom of Buganda in the 1860s. Anglican missionaries came from Britain, while their Catholic counterparts tended to originate in France. The message of both sets of missionaries soon spread to the rest of what would become Uganda, marking a turning point in the religious life of the people, particularly the Baganda, as well as in the political structure of the Buganda kingdom and the region at large. As Christian doctrine denounced all native religious behavior and practices as heathen and satanic, becoming a Christian meant breaking away completely from one's old lifestyle and adjusting to new moral and religious standards. New believers, called *abalokole* (ah-ba-LO-KO-li), were regarded as social rebels who had transferred their loyalty to a new religious system, thus turning their backs on their tribal traditions and their communities. This prompted several decades of strife and bloodshed between Christians and adherents to traditional religions. Christian converts, with the support of the missionaries and their connections to the British military, were able to divide the Buganda kingdom and rule it through a puppet king dependent on their support. In response, traditionalists carried out campaigns of violence against Christian converts, executing twenty-six Christians in one incident in 1886. Rather than extinguish the spread of Christianity, the martyrdom of these believers seemed to spark its growth, and Christians received favored status under the British protectorate.

Christianity enjoyed a revival in the 1980s, though it had long-term consequences for some of Uganda's minorities. In the wake of the violence caused by Idi Amin and the civil war, Western Christian groups filled much of the void left by the unstable government. Christian groups provided medical care and education to the Ugandan people, binding them together when it seemed like events were conspiring to tear them apart. The Ugandan people looked on these groups positively as a result, since their actions were quite literally saving lives. Over the course of the next two decades, increasingly fundamentalist Christian figures began entering Uganda, mostly from the United States, with the aim of fostering a widespread acceptance of their incredibly strict interpretation of the religion. Since these groups were also spending millions on schools, hospitals, and orphanages, the Ugandan people went along with their teachings.

The conservative beliefs handed down for generations among rural Ugandans also played a role in these fundamentalist figures gaining a following. For their part, men like Scott Lively or Tony Perkins were turning to Africa because the radical views they preached had largely fallen out of the mainstream in the United States, and Africa was a place where they could still draw an audience. The most pernicious effect of these figures coming to Uganda was the increasing intolerance for the country's LGBT population. Preachers (including some native Ugandan preachers like Robert Kayanja and Martin Ssempa) demonized the country's gay residents and advocated for the passage of anti-homosexual laws. Their antiquated attitudes regarding sex and sexuality also hampered the fight against HIV/AIDS, as they discouraged the use of contraceptives and fostered a climate in which gay men feared coming forward and getting tested. Happily, these fundamentalists are not representative of the totality of Christian leadership in Uganda. Many preachers have spoken out against the American extremists and their followers, and have encouraged education

Christian churches have been a common sight in Uganda since the religion was brought to the country by missionaries in the late nineteenth century.

Led by Joseph Kony, the Lord's Resistance Army (LRA) is a far-right paramilitary organization that terrorized northern Uganda for two decades from the 1980s through the 2000s. The group follows an extremist interpretation of Christianity and claims to want a government based on the Ten Commandments of the Bible. LRA activities led to the death or displacement of nearly two million people, in addition to other crimes, including rape and child slavery. The group has now been degraded to the point that it no longer poses an active threat to Uganda, but Kony remains at large.

about sexual health and contraceptive use. Others, including Reverend Kapya Kaoma and the Anglican bishop Christopher Senyonjo, have been driven from their churches because of their vocal support for the country's gay population.

ISLAM, HINDUSIM, AND JUDAISM

Christopher Senyonjo has actively supported the country's LGBT population and has endured consequences as a result.

While the vast majority of Ugandans today are Christians, there are minority religious communities throughout the country. After Christianity, Islam is the most prevalent religion in the nation. Islam was brought to Uganda by traders from the Arab world in the mid-nineteenth century; some of the Muslims in the country today are the descendants of those very traders. Others have emigrated over the years from Muslim-majority nations in the region. Most major Ugandan cities today have at least one mosque. Muslims were favored under the rule of Idi Amin, who was a member of the faith himself and banned evangelical Christianity during his time in power. The number of Muslims in Uganda grew significantly while he was in control of the country.

Most of Uganda's Hindus came from the Indian subcontinent during the colonial era, migrating from one British possession to another. In Uganda, the Hindu community opened stores, ran businesses, and handled banking, all of which they did very successfully. Idi Amin subsequently expelled most of them in the 1970s, prompting an economic collapse. Hindu places of worship were largely untouched, however, allowing the community to rebuild after Amin was removed from power. There is once again a small Hindu community in

Uganda today, with Hindu temples active places of worship and an accepted part of the country's religious landscape.

In eastern Uganda there is a community of Ugandans known as the Abayudaya, who practice Judaism. They observe Jewish holidays and dietary laws, sing Hebrew songs, and keep the Sabbath holy, as Jews have for generations. This all started in the early part of the twentieth century, when a well-known Baganda leader named Semei Kakungulu resisted both the European colonialists and the missionaries with whom he came into contact. Kakungulu read of the Jewish faith, met several European Jews working in the British protectorate, and was eager to read, learn, and practice the religion. During the 1920s, a European Jewish trader met Kakungulu and taught his community the theory and practice of Judaism. In 1992, two Americans visited the Abayudaya for the Sabbath and were urged to send more visitors. Since then, many more have visited the isolated community, including two rabbis and a delegation of American Jews. It is a very small community, estimated in 2009 to number just 1,100 people, but it is indicative of the religious diversity in Uganda, as well as the tolerance of multiple faiths by the country's government and people.

Uganda's minority Muslim population worships at mosques throughout the country.

INTERNET LINKS

https://dacb.org/histories/uganda-history-christianity
This page contains a wealth of information about the history of Christianity in Uganda, including extensive discussions of its society-altering role in the early colonial period.

https://globalpressjournal.com/africa/uganda/ugandans-mix -traditional-beliefs-religion-now-open-practice
This article from the *Global Press Journal* profiles Ugandans of mixed faiths, who incorporate traditional tribal religions with Christianity or Islam.

LANGUAGE

Ugandans communicate with one another in dozens of languages, but Swahili, English, and Luganda are the most prominent.

AS A RESULT OF THE MANY TRIBES and ethnic groups within Uganda's borders, thirty-eight different languages are spoken throughout the country. Of these, English and Swahili are the most prevalent, and both are recognized as national languages. English is the language of business and the government, and access to economic and political power is almost impossible without having mastered it. Outside of major towns and cities, however, it is not widely used. Swahili is far more common as a trade language among individual Ugandans. Luganda is also an important tongue spoken by the large Baganda population.

"It is true that in Uganda we speak many languages. But difference of languages is no difficulty at all in the unity of Uganda."
—Milton Obote

LUGANDA

While English is the language of the powerful, and Swahili the language of the masses, Luganda is the language of the Baganda. Luganda is spoken

Ugandan schools currently teach English to all of their students, as English is the principal language used in courts of law and in most businesses. During the 1970s, language instruction focused more on Arabic and Swahili, as Arabic was the language used by Idi Amin's government and Swahili was commonly spoken by members of the upper class. Since Amin's fall from power, however, English is now the language of the powerful, and it is very difficult to acquire any kind of wealth or influence without speaking it.

from the northwest shore of Lake Victoria and the Tanzanian border to Lake Kyoga in the center of the country. It developed over many centuries as a spoken language but has existed in written form only since the arrival of the Arabs and the Europeans in the nineteenth century. At first, Luganda words did not have any fixed spelling, which made the language difficult to read. In 1947, a conference was held to standardize the language; it now has a clearly determined form based on five vowel sounds and twenty-one consonants. Luganda has both long and short consonant sounds, like the Japanese language.

LOCAL LANGUAGES

The other languages spoken in Uganda are used mainly in local areas among specific ethnic and tribal communities. These languages are occasionally taught in local primary schools, and they are used for targeted campaigns (such as those promoting birth control or literacy) and on radio programs created for people living in a specific area.

Languages among the tribal groups include Lusoga, which is spoken by the Basoga, and Lugwere, spoken by the Bagwe people. Acholi is spoken by 4 percent of the population, mainly in the north-central Acholi district, while Dhopadhola is the most distinct of the Western Nilotic languages in Uganda.

Of the non-Ugandan languages, Hindi and Gujarati are commonly spoken among members of the South Asian Hindu community that migrated to Uganda during the early part of the twentieth century. They are also commonly used in newspapers and radio programs produced for these populations.

UGANDAN NAMES

Names are very important in Uganda, as they indicate tribal and religious affiliations, and sometimes signify what clan an individual belongs to. Due to religious influences, however, most people in Uganda have an Arab or European name, which is more commonly used than his or her traditional name.

Traditional names are unique to particular places and tribes. Simply by mentioning one's name, most Ugandans will know to which tribe an individual belongs. Names are often handed down from generation to generation. They can also relate to the appearance of a child at birth, or reflect wishes for what he or she will grow up to be, such as Makula (ma-KOO-la), which means "beauty." Most common of all is simply to call the child by the name of the day on which he or she was born, such as Balaza (ba-LA-za), meaning "Monday." Sometimes chosen names are the names of gods or spirits, reflecting the traditional beliefs of the area in which the child was born. Circumstances prevailing in the tribe at the time of someone's birth can give rise to other names, such as Lutalo (loo-TA-lo), meaning "war," or Mirembe (mee-REM-bay), meaning "peace."

Multiple births give rise to special names, which vary from tribe to tribe. The Baganda, for instance, use Babirye and Nakato for girls, and Wasswa and Kato for boys. At the birth of twins, it is quite common for the father and mother to take on new names as well. The name Nalongo indicates the mother of twins, and Salongo the father.

JOURNALISM AND THE MEDIA

Uganda is home to a robust media environment, with numerous print, radio, and television outlets. Dozens of newspapers are printed daily in multiple languages, with the highest circulation belonging to the state-owned *New Vision*. Privately owned papers include the *Daily Monitor* and the *Observer*. There are also over 150 radio stations in the country, which broadcast in more than twenty languages. The government-owned Uganda Broadcasting Corporation (UBC) operates five stations, with the rest privately owned and operated. Also available in the country are BBC World Service and Radio France Internationale. Many Ugandans own a radio, even in rural parts of the

In Uganda, there is an altered version of English called Ugandan English. A common feature of this language is clumsily translated Ugandan proverbs. One popular example is a justification of official corruption: "Man eateth where he worketh."

Uganda's press includes a wide variety of newspapers.

country, and listening to broadcasts is a popular pastime. Televisions are less commonly found, as they are much more expensive. Villages will occasionally have a communal television located in a common area, around which villagers will gather to watch the news or other programming. There is one government-run channel, as well as dozens of other local and satellite stations. Programs are mainly in English, Swahili, and Luganda, and run twenty-four hours a day. Digital satellite television is also available in the country, marketed to those Ugandans who can afford it by companies located in Tanzania, Kenya, South Africa, and China. Netflix became available in Uganda in 2016, but its usage is limited. Many Ugandans lack televisions or other devices capable of accessing the service, and the cost of internet access fast enough to handle extensive video streaming is often more than the average citizen can afford.

While Uganda appears to be a role model for a healthy, open media culture, free expression is being increasingly restricted by the government. Though the constitution provides for a free press, journalists are regularly targeted by the state for coverage that is hostile to the government's interests. Reporters Without Borders lists "grave attacks on the media" in the country, citing almost daily acts of violence and intimidation carried out against reporters. Journalists that expose governmental corruption are arrested arbitrarily by the police, and criticism of Museveni's government can be met with beatings, abductions, or confiscation of equipment. Reporters are threatened with treason charges in an effort to silence them, and laws covering broadcast codes are selectively applied by the government to throttle hostile outlets. The offices of the *Observer* were broken into twice between 2016 and 2018, with computers and security camera footage confiscated each time. A special team of state security officers was also formed in 2017 to scour social media for criticism of the government. The internet has been disconnected and access blocked to social media sites during elections, a transparent attempt at voter suppression.

In July 2018, a tax went into effect on the use of sixty popular mobile apps, including Facebook, Instagram, Twitter, and WhatsApp. The tax charges 200 shillings (roughly a nickel in US currency) a day for access to the apps, effectively doubling what it costs for Ugandans to access the internet. Both Ugandan citizens and international organizations have called this a clear attempt to silence speech and reduce access to forums for people to exchange information, particularly among the poor. The tax follows similar laws in Tanzania and Egypt, and Museveni has justified its existence by calling social media platforms a "luxury" and arguing that it will discourage "gossip." Protests against the tax were met with tear gas and arrests, and despite the valiant efforts of the measure's opponents, early reports have indicated that the tax is having the desired effect. A survey found that 71 percent of Ugandans had been extremely inconvenienced in accessing social media, and had therefore been using those platforms less.

When pressed on these issues, the government points to the variety of media outlets in the country as proof of its open journalistic culture. This is misleading, however. Just because press outlets are allowed to remain open does not mean they can criticize those in power without facing repercussions. Museveni's attacks on the press and his attempts to suppress dissent are an indicator of the increasingly antidemocratic nature of his rule. They will likely escalate as Ugandans grow more frustrated with his clinging to power.

INTERNET LINKS

https://languagesgulper.com/eng/Swahili.html
This site provides a profile of the Swahili language, including its origin, its various dialects across the African continent, and its grammatical structure.

http://www.monitor.co.ug
The *Daily Monitor* is the most popular privately owned newspaper in Uganda, providing coverage of politics, business, culture, sports, and international affairs.

ARTS

Decorative baskets are just one example of the many traditional pieces of craftwork made in Uganda.

10

DESPITE THE HARDSHIPS MANY FACE in their daily lives, the Ugandan people have maintained a commitment to artistic expression. Through performance and practical skill, writing and speaking, Ugandan artists have communicated their experiences through a variety of mediums. Literature, music, and dance have long histories in Uganda, while a film industry is just getting off the ground. Craftspeople are responsible for making highly decorative mats, baskets, pots, and chairs, and fine artists cater to a select clientele. Though government investment in the arts is nearly nonexistent, this has not prevented Ugandan artists from pursuing their dreams and banding together to produce works of enduring importance.

● ● ● ● ● ● ● ● ● ● ● ● ● ● ●

"Art can be a tool of political activism … I can cause change in someone by capturing an emotion in a picture or painting." –Nuwa Wamala Nnyanzi, artist

LITERATURE

Storytelling in Uganda goes back hundreds of years, as all of the country's tribes have oral traditions that have been passed down from generation to generation. Written stories are a more recent innovation, however, as the tribes lacked written languages. With the coming of the English language, stories began to be recorded, and a literary culture soon developed. Uganda had one of the most vibrant literary scenes in all of Africa in the 1960s. The literary journal *Transition Magazine: An International Review* was founded in 1961 by Rajat Neogy and continues to publish today. Makerere University also hosted the first African Writers Conference in 1962, which counted Chinua Achebe, Wole Soyinka, and Langston Hughes among its many attendees. *Transition* printed work by Achebe, James Baldwin, and Julius Nyerere, but political events soon began to push writers out of the country. The political turmoil of Obote's two presidencies and the Amin dictatorship in between forced many intellectuals to flee the country, fearing for their lives.

Transition Magazine has published the works of some of the most prominent writers and intellectuals from Africa and across the diaspora since its founding in 1961.

The oral tradition persisted during this time, however, and has been a major influence on the works that have made up the modern Ugandan literary renaissance. Building on the work of earlier writers, including the poet Okot p'Bitek, much of Ugandan literature is now written knowing that its audience is more accustomed to hearing stories than reading them. "Listening to Poetry," by Ngobi Kagayi, is one such poem.

There is a growing number of female writers in Uganda. Many write about HIV/AIDS, homosexuality, or gender-based violence from a perspective that is rarely heard from elsewhere in society. These subjects are somewhat taboo in Uganda and can be explored through literature in a way that may not otherwise be possible. Other authors have been able to process their trauma from growing up amid violence, either from the civil war or from the fighting with the Lord's Resistance Army, through literature, and they have helped other Ugandans work through their own experiences.

Many female authors, including Mary Karooro Okurut, Doreen Baingana, and Beatrice Lamwaka, have also worked with, or seen their work published by,

There is a strong tradition of storytelling among the many tribal groups in Uganda, in which stories are passed down orally from grandparents to grandchildren as part of the child's education. These stories have survived intact for centuries, and Ugandan children still love to listen to the elders of the family retell them in the same manner they were told a generation before. Although some of these stories are very old, they were not written down until quite recently, as none of the tribes had a written language. For this reason, it is difficult to know the origin of many of the stories. Most surviving tales are directed at children and have a clear moral, and a great number of them feature talking animals. Some of these animals are good characters that help children, but others are designed to be frightening and warn the children of the consequences of behaving badly. Curiously, a bearlike creature features as a scary monster in many of the tales, despite the fact that there are no bears in Uganda. Two of the best-known stories are "Nabweteme" ("The Forest"), which shows the value of being courageous under difficult circumstances, and "Jogoli Jogoli" ("Disrespect"), which illustrates the importance of listening to the instructions of one's parents.

FEMRITE, the Uganda Women Writers Association. Established in the mid-1990s by Okurut, the organization was founded to help increase literacy rates among Ugandan women and help female authors get their work published. Since traditional gender roles dictate that women are not supposed to talk about their own feelings, much of the organization's work involves empowering women to feel confident enough to come forward with stories of their own. Over the last twenty years, FEMRITE has published nearly fifty books, including novels, poetry anthologies, and nonfiction works. It has also expanded throughout East Africa and has begun focusing on larger political issues.

The Ugandan novelist and politician Mary Karooro Okurut speaks at Girl Summit in London, England, in 2014..

Creating a new generation of writers in Uganda has been difficult over the last thirty years. Millions of people were displaced by the political instability that rocked the country, a situation that continued in the areas of the country targeted by the LRA. Many Ugandans are illiterate, and many more lack the time or opportunity to write or publish anything. Schools are overcrowded,

Tropical Fish: Stories Out of Entebbe *by Doreen Baingana (short stories)*
Abyssinian Chronicles *by Moses Isegawa*
Trials and Tribulations in Sandu's Home *by Godfrey Kalimugogo*
Child Soldier: Fighting for My Life *by China Keitetsi (memoir)*
Kintu *by Jennifer Nansubuga Makumbi*
Song for the Sun in Us *by Okello Oculi (poetry)*
The Invisible Weevil *by Mary Karooro Okurut*

and much of their curricula remain stuck in models developed by the British during the colonial period; this means that children are only exposed to the classics of English literature and rarely read anything written by Ugandans. There are also few bookstores and no door-to-door postal service in many parts of the country, preventing interested readers from receiving books or magazines through the mail. Despite these factors, FEMRITE and other organizations like it have been successful in both advocating for educational improvements and finding and amplifying unique voices. This will hopefully inspire other storytellers to take up the pen and add their own perspectives to the cultural conversation.

POPULAR MUSIC

Music is very important in Uganda, and musicians are often the biggest local celebrities. Native artists use their songs to relay messages promoting economic and social change. They sing mostly in Luganda or Swahili, the languages of the people. Some artists also sing in English, as foreign music is popular within the country, and Ugandans are used to hearing English-language lyrics.

In the past, music was mostly played on a few simple instruments, including the lyre, the marimba, the thumb piano, and the drum. Drums were used as instruments of communication as well, particularly in dances, ceremonies, and tribal rituals. The lyrics of older Ugandan songs focused on family, legends, and well-known historical events, and were often used as a form of storytelling, incorporating both a lead singer and a chorus that would reply in unison.

In modern Uganda, music both foreign and domestic is regularly heard, and genres unique to Uganda have begun to emerge. Music from South Africa, the Democratic Republic of the Congo, and the United States is blasted from radios across Uganda and has influenced the styles of local artists. *Kidandali* music, the most popular genre in the country, grew out of Congolese and Afrobeat big band styles, and is marked by its upbeat tempo and full sound. Afrigo Band, the first group in Uganda to release its music on CD, performs this style of music, as does Bobi Wine. Wine's popularity as a musician was an important factor in his successful run for Parliament in 2017.

One of the most popular musicians and politicians in Uganda is Bobi Wine. Here he performs in Busabala, a suburb of Kampala, in November 2018.

Closely related to *kidandali* is dancehall music, which bears Jamaican influences. Dancehall music became popular in the 1990s and is usually sung in local languages. There are many discos and nightclubs in Uganda in which it can be heard, either prerecorded or live. American hip-hop has influenced not only Ugandan music but also styles of dress and patterns of speech. This genre gained popularity in the late 2000s, and the term "Lugaflow" has been coined to describe hip-hop sung in the Luganda language. Notable hip-hop artists include Keko and Navio.

Kadongo kamu music is more closely related to Uganda's traditional songwriting. Meaning "one guitar" in Luganda, *kadongo kamu* features a more stripped-down sound and is predominantly found in the Buganda region. Well-known artists include Fred Masagazi, Christophe Sebaguka, and Dan Mugalula. Other popular genres include gospel and R&B, the latter of which lets artists experiment with languages and rhythms in ways that other styles of music do not allow. While Ugandan musicians sing from the heart and try to speak to the realities of life in Uganda, the industry is still very informal, and artists earn little money from album sales. Most of their income is made through live shows at bars, clubs, or other venues.

Robert Kyagulanyi, who performs under the name Bobi Wine, is a popular musician of the kidandali *genre who was elected to Parliament in 2017. His songs often address political and social issues, and he is particularly popular with young people, who feel that his music expresses the fears and frustrations of their daily lives. Wine's 2017 song "Freedom" questions the legitimacy of Yoweri Museveni's presidency and argues that Uganda's current government is restricting the rights of its citizens and moving the country in the wrong direction. The song is sung in multiple languages, and urges Ugandans from across the country to come together to defend their freedoms.*

> *We are fed up of those who oppress our lives*
> *And everything that takes away our rights.*
> *Uganda seems to be moving backwards.*
> *This is almost making us hate our own nation.*
>
> ...
>
> *Where is my freedom of expression,*
> *When you judge me because of my expression?*
> *Look what you're doing to this nation.*
> *What are you teaching the future generation?*
> *See our leaders become misleaders*
> *And see our mentors become tormentors.*
> *Freedom fighters become dictators.*
> *They look 'pon the youth and say we're destructors.*
> —Bobi Wine, "Freedom"

TRADITIONAL DANCES

Dances in Uganda are a way of celebrating important events. As with the prevalent cultures and languages, similarities between certain dances are usually indicative of their regional origins. Even the smallest variation in the dance, however, can alter its entire meaning and can allow an experienced observer to identify both the particular tribe and the occasion for the dance. Whether for marriage, birth, royalty, or death, every type of dance is still important today in many parts of Uganda.

The Baganda tribe has many traditional dances, including *mbaga* (m-BAG-ah) and *nankasa* (nan-KA-sa). The *mbaga* dance honors important ceremonies, such as weddings and royal gatherings, where the women and men often dance together in a choreographed manner. *Nankasa* is a popular dance performed on almost all other, less official occasions.

The Bagisu are famous for their circumcision dance, *embalu* (em-BAA-loo). The men dance in a circle around their friends about to enter manhood, while the women dance around the circle with encouraging comments of bravery. Most relatives take part in this lively and enthusiastic dance. The Acholi have eight communal dances, held to mark ceremonial occasions, funerals, or successful hunts, or to ensure victory in battle.

CRAFTS AND FINE ARTS

The practice and appreciation of fine arts are limited to a small but expanding segment of the population. The School of Fine Arts at Makerere University has trained some of East Africa's leading painters, sculptors, and art teachers. The school also teaches industrial art and design. Nuwa Wamala Nnyanzi, an artist who has held exhibitions in the United States and South Africa, says that the lack of government support for the arts is a major barrier in developing a wider audience. Uganda does not provide any subsidies for its artists or have any major national galleries or other government-organized collections of art; this is a legacy of Idi Amin's rule, which saw many museums looted and occupied. There is also little art education offered in Ugandan schools, which discourages children from developing an appreciation for the arts and pursuing any interest they may have in the field. Poverty is another obvious culprit in preventing many Ugandans from having any time to devote to artistic expression or appreciation.

Nnyanzi started painting in Kenya in 1978 after fleeing from the Amin regime. He specializes in pastels, acrylics, oils, watercolors, and batik, a textile

Nuwa Wamala Nnyanzi has been producing art of various kinds in Uganda and East Africa for more than four decades.

FILM IN UGANDA

Though Uganda has no formal film industry as of yet, that has not stopped enterprising filmmakers from writing, directing, and exhibiting movies. The most well-known filmmaker in Uganda is Isaac Nabwana, the man behind Ramon Productions. Inspired by American action movies while growing up in the Wakaliga slum on the outskirts of Kampala, Nabwana (who directs under the name Nabwana IGG) now makes bloody action movies on incredibly low budgets. Entirely self-taught, Nabwana borrowed a camera from a neighbor, scavenged props from the slum in which he lived, put together a small cast and crew of volunteers, and began writing and shooting films in the late 2000s. The films cost about $200 US to make, and they heavily feature the slums, as Nabwana knows his audience will want to see a world that it recognizes. The films also feature car chases, helicopter raids, zombies, and shoot-outs. The violence is stylized and deliberately over-the-top, as Nabwana does not want to faithfully recreate the types of violence that he and most of his film's viewers will have personally experienced. His home (which he built by hand) doubles as a studio and rehearsal space, and many of his cast and crew sleep there at the end of the day, since they have no homes of their own.

He has so far produced over a dozen films, with Operation Kakongoliro! The Ugandan Expendables *his most ambitious project yet, boasting a budget of $2,000. Nabwana's wife is his co-editor and also helps in distributing the films.*

Since there are no movie theaters in the slums, the films are distributed on DVD. The cast and crew go door-to-door to sell copies of the latest movie, and they split the profits with the director.

Nabwana has inspired other independent filmmakers in Uganda, and there are now over five hundred film production companies in the country. Though the industry is still in its very earliest stages and has no regulation or oversight as of yet, the future looks bright. The Uganda Film Festival was inaugurated in 2013, and since that time both the quality and quantity of films produced in Uganda have increased.

painting technique introduced to Uganda by Southeast Asian immigrants. He describes his art as expressive, yet with a linear language, and the colors of his paintings are earthy and alive, reflective of African culture and the environment. He says the role of the artist is to hold a mirror up to society and to comment on what he sees. He is also optimistic about the future, saying

ALL THE WORLD'S A STAGE

There is a rich theater tradition in Uganda, at both the national and local levels. In the twenty-first century, it has played a crucial role in educating the public about gender issues, domestic violence, and the spread of HIV/AIDS. One organization is the Girl Up Initiative. This group uses performance art such as music, dance, and theater to promote awareness about issues affecting women around the country. Key concepts are sexual and reproductive rights and health as well as gender-based violence. Delivering messages in this way enables people, especially younger people, to connect to and empathize with the situations presented, allowing them to be shaped and molded and to take action in the future.

that children are more exposed to art than ever before, thanks to the internet, and are embracing their Ugandan culture. With any luck, this will lead to a new generation of artists who will continue to reflect Ugandan society through their own personal mirrors for many years to come.

INTERNET LINKS

https://femrite.org
FEMRITE, the Uganda Women Writers Association, provides information about the history of the group and its publications, details on the work it is carrying out in both Uganda and the wider East African region, and the dates of upcoming literary events.

https://globalpressjournal.com/africa/uganda/one-hour-uganda -one-mans-dream-preserve-ugandan-culture-traditional-dance -music-food
This article discusses dance traditions in Uganda, as well as the efforts being made to preserve tribal dances for a new generation of Ugandans.

LEISURE

Soccer is an extremely popular sport among Ugandans of all ages.

11

"One who sees something good must narrate it."
—Ugandan proverb

THOUGH MANY UGANDANS ARE kept busy by various forms of labor for much of their days, there are periods where they are able to relax and enjoy a bit of leisure time. How this leisure time is spent is largely determined by whether a particular individual lives in the city or the country, and how much money he or she has. Residents in rural villages, where many homes lack electricity, are more likely to spend their leisure time visiting neighbors or playing simple games. For those with more money, downtime may also be occupied by listening to the radio or watching television. In the cities, Ugandans engage in activities more familiar to Westerners, like going to nightclubs, discos, or swimming pools. Sports are also a popular pastime among Ugandans of all classes, particularly soccer and boxing.

LEISURE IN THE VILLAGES

Children in less wealthy parts of Uganda amuse themselves with whatever items are found in their neighborhoods—in this case, an old tire.

Entertainment in Ugandan villages is largely derived from personal interactions. Friends, family, and neighbors meet up with one another and talk about their children, their fields, or politics. Since many rural Ugandans lack disposable income, they are largely responsible for entertaining themselves, and they take pleasure in others' company. Storytelling is a popular pastime for this reason, as children (and other adults) listen while their elders recount fables or tales from their youth. Some of these traditional tales may have changed slightly over the years, but their core themes remain the same. The communal storytelling experience has been transformed in some villages by the advent of radios and televisions, which have replaced traditional storytellers as the point of focus for community gatherings. Ugandans in these villages gather around to watch or listen to the latest program or sporting event, and to collectively react to it.

Ugandan children still enjoy the games played by their parents when they were young, using little more than ropes, corncobs, leaves, and earth to keep themselves entertained. Dirt building is played by teams of small children. Each team has a group of small red seeds from the *olasiti* tree that are hidden in a long mound of dirt. This mound is then divided into several smaller piles, and the opposing team guesses in which pile the seeds are hidden. If a team guesses correctly, it takes charge of the game. If not, this is counted as a score against them.

LEISURE IN THE CITIES

Urban Ugandans, especially the wealthy, have far more leisure options than their rural countrymen. With peace restored to the country, the last few decades have seen an increase in recreational facilities within the cities, including movie theaters, where international as well as African films are shown; shopping malls; and bowling alleys. Kampala also has a theme park, the Wonder World Amusement Park. There are swimming pools and a few soccer stadiums, and, for Uganda's wealthier citizens, fancy clubs that allow

DINING OUT

Although food is important in Ugandan tradition, eating out is not nearly as common as having friends or family over for a meal at home. Restaurants are mostly visited by workers at lunchtime or out for business meetings, and by tourists visiting the country.

members to play golf, squash, or tennis. For the poorest slum dwellers, leisure activities are largely the same as those in the villages.

Uganda's largest cities and towns also have a bustling nightlife. In places with regular access to electricity, nightclubs, discos, dance halls, and casinos are extremely popular venues, and many stay open almost all night long. Bars and pubs host live music and local dancers, while larger nightclubs feature live DJs and special sound systems. The music played is a mixture of African and international dancehall and pop. Some bars and clubs are deliberately Western in nature, in an effort to attract tourists looking for familiar food, drink, and atmosphere.

In Uganda's cities, nightclubs and bars provide opportunities to drink, play games, and socialize.

Going out as a family is not a Ugandan tradition—this is more common in the Western world. In Uganda, women and children tend to go off in one direction while their husbands and fathers go off in another. The older members of the community have little need for modern forms of entertainment and are happy to sit and talk in quiet settings, discussing subjects like politics, religion, and family. Men and women of this age group usually sit separately in social environments.

THE SPORTING LIFE

Many Ugandans are avid sportsmen and sportswomen. The most popular sport in the country is soccer, known as football in Uganda. It is played in schools, villages, and towns by men and women at all levels of society. In the villages, it is typically played in friendly fashion among informal teams, while in the towns matches tend to be more organized and played between semi-official

Ugandan athletes have won a total of seven medals at the Summer Olympic Games. The first gold medal was won by John Akii-Bua in the men's 400-meter hurdles at the 1972 Games in Munich. Another gold was taken by Stephen Kiprotich in the men's marathon at the 2012 London Games. Boxing has historically been the best event for Ugandan athletes, earning the country four medals (three silvers and a bronze), but the sport has not produced a medalist since 1980. Uganda has not yet participated in a Winter Olympics.

The Uganda national soccer team poses for a photo before a World Cup qualifying Group E match in 2016.

clubs. There are also a few professional soccer stadiums in Uganda, including Mandela National Stadium just outside of Kampala, the home of the Uganda national soccer team (known as the Cranes). Amateur players are content to practice on any field or clearing around their towns or homesteads. Soccer is also popular as a spectator sport, and many Ugandan soccer fans watch international matches between top European teams on television. Young boys can often be seen wearing the colors of their favorite team.

Boxing was especially popular in the 1970s during the dictatorship of Idi Amin, who was himself a boxer in his youth. During this period, Uganda produced several world champions, including Leo Rwabwogo, Ayub Kalule, and John Mugabi. Boxing has declined in popularity in recent years, however, partly as a result of the long-term injuries suffered by many boxers.

Netball is tremendously popular among schoolgirls in Uganda. The game is similar to basketball and is played by opposing teams of seven players each, with the aim of getting a ball in the opposing team's goal ring as many times as possible. The netball court is divided by two lines, and at each end of the court is a shooting semicircle and a 10-foot (3 m) goalpost with no backboard. Scoring shots can be taken only from within this semicircle. Each team member has a designated position that is restricted to a specific area of the court. These restricted areas have both an attacking and a defending player in them, one from each opposing team. The team that scores the most goals is the winner, and netball games last for one hour.

Other popular sports in Uganda include swimming, tennis, golf, squash, rugby, and cricket. Though Uganda's citizens enjoy playing these sports, both professionally and for pleasure, the Ugandan government has shown little interest in investing in its nation's athletes. Idi Amin was the last Ugandan leader to take sports seriously, and since then the country's athletic community has languished, largely unable to achieve international success. Investments at the school level, to ensure that schoolchildren have access to playgrounds and rudimentary athletic facilities, would go a long way to developing a pool of athletic talent in the country. Scholarships for athletes from poor backgrounds would also provide opportunities for children that might not otherwise leave their rural communities. Ugandans have a passion for sports, and investments in them would both improve the lives of Uganda's citizens and bring economic and reputational benefits to the country.

INTERNET LINKS

http://www.cayennekampala.com
The Cayenne Restaurant & Lounge is a popular venue in Kampala that features a poolside bar, a dance floor, and a menu filled with international cuisine.

https://www.fufa.co.ug/uganda-cranes
This profile of the Uganda Cranes, the country's national soccer team, contains a history of the organization, performance records, and information about the team's current roster of players.

http://www.monitor.co.ug/Sports/690254-690254-cprrey/index.html
The sports page of the *Daily Monitor* provides relevant, up-to-date coverage of sports in Uganda and around Africa as a whole.

FESTIVALS

Parades and other festivals are held on a wide variety
of occasions throughout the year in Uganda.

THROUGHOUT THE YEAR, Ugandans celebrate numerous holidays and hold a wide variety of festivals. Some, including Christmas, Easter, and Eid al-Fitr, are religious holidays observed by members of Uganda's various faiths. Other holidays, such as Liberation Day or Independence Day, are secular and honor important dates in Ugandan history. Festivals are held to mark important moments in a particular citizen's life, including birth, marriage, and death. These festivals often include traditional tribal ceremonies that are still practiced in many parts of the country.

RELIGIOUS AND SECULAR HOLIDAYS

Christians and Muslims in Uganda celebrate the traditional holidays of their faiths in much the same way as other Christians and Muslims around the world. Christians exchange gifts on Christmas and have large family gatherings on Easter, and attend church services on both days. Ugandan Muslims observe the fasting month of Ramadan and mark its conclusion

12

Martyrs' Day, commemorated on June 3 by Christians in Uganda, honors the forty-five Christian converts—twenty-two Catholics and twenty-three Anglicans—who were killed between 1885 and 1887 at the orders of the kabaka of Buganda, Mwanga II, after they refused to denounce their faith.

IMPORTANT HOLIDAYS IN UGANDA

January 1. . . . . .New Year's Day
January 26 . . . . .Liberation Day
February 16 . . . .Archbishop Janani Luwum Day
Date Varies . . . .Easter
March 8 . . . . . .International Women's Day
May 1. . . . . . . .International Labor Day
May 25 . . . . . . .Africa Day
June 3. . . . . . . .Martyrs' Day
June 9. . . . . . . .National Heroes Day
Date Varies . . . .Eid al-Fitr
October 9. . . . . .Independence Day
Date Varies . . . .Eid al-Adha
December 25. . . .Christmas Day
December 26. . . .Boxing Day

Here, Ugandan Muslims celebrate Mawlid al-Nabi, the birthday of the prophet Muhammad.

with the feast of Eid al-Fitr. Feasts are also held on Eid al-Adha, which commemorates the Quranic account of Ibrahim's willingness to sacrifice his son Ishmael at Allah's command. Muslims also attend mosque on this day, and some sacrifice an animal and share a portion of its meat with the poor.

There are also numerous secular holidays in Uganda, including Liberation Day, Independence Day, Africa Day, and National Heroes Day. Liberation Day, celebrated on January 26, commemorates the coming to power of the National Resistance Movement (NRM) in 1986. On this day, the president typically gives a public speech on the state of the nation. Independence Day, which takes place on October 9, marks the date that Uganda was granted full political sovereignty in 1962. Africa Day is observed on May 25 across the continent of Africa. It celebrates the

ARCHBISHOP JANANI LUWUM DAY

Held every year on February 16, Archbishop Janani Luwum Day celebrates the life of Janani Luwum, the former archbishop of the Anglican Church of Uganda. Archbishop Luwum was an outspoken critic of Idi Amin during the 1970s who protested against the dictator's disappearances and murders of his political enemies. In response, Amin had the archbishop arrested and murdered. The public holiday honoring the archbishop's memory was inaugurated in 2016.

foundation of the Organization of African Unity (OAU), now the African Union. It also symbolizes the ongoing progress being made by Africans in achieving true self-determination and popular rule. National Heroes Day, held on June 9, was instituted in 2001 to honor those who played important roles in creating a better future for Ugandans. In the morning, wreaths are laid on the graves of innocent victims of the country's civil war, and in the afternoon, heroes are awarded medals by the government. Uganda also recognizes International Women's Day on March 8, and International Labor Day on May 1. All of these occasions, with the exception of Africa Day, are public holidays, with schools and most businesses closed.

TRADITIONAL FESTIVALS

The crucial stages of life—birth, puberty, marriage, death—have always been times of sacred importance to Ugandans, as they signify changes in the status of an individual and that person's relationship with his or her fellow members of society. In rural areas, these important events are celebrated with traditional festivals, which vary based on the particular tribe and area of the country. In large towns and cities, these occasions are celebrated in a more Western manner.

CUSTOMS OF BIRTH

While the naming of a newborn child can take place at a variety of times after the birth, it is always an important reason to celebrate. Sometimes this celebration is held immediately after the child is delivered, though it can also be delayed until a time when all of the newborn's relatives can get together for a party with plenty of food, singing, and dancing. In Christian families, the child is usually welcomed as a new member of the local church, as well as through the sacrament of baptism. This form of celebration, the contemporary christening ceremony, is performed regularly in Uganda for Christian families.

CUSTOMS OF MARRIAGE

The rite of passage of marriage is celebrated with many festivals in Uganda. These ceremonies are often accompanied by feasting and gift giving to express the pride of the community in the happy couple. The wedding festival welcomes the newlyweds into successful participation in the community, and celebrates the community's future expansion through the birth of children. Among most tribes, dancing and feasting after the wedding last well into the following day. The food is simple—meat stew with rice or corn—but plentiful, and is eaten outdoors. Within certain tribes, it is customary to present large wedding gifts (up to and including a marital bed, complete with new linen, pillows, and a bedspread) at the reception for the guests to admire. Modern-day city weddings take the form of a religious service followed by a large reception for family and friends at home or at one of the many hotels in Kampala. This is a fairly formal occasion, at which a grand buffet is served to the guests. Many couples in Uganda opt to combine these traditions, holding both a Christian wedding ceremony and a traditional tribal wedding.

CUSTOMS OF DEATH

Traditional funerals in Uganda include the playing of alternately mournful and joyful music, as well as the making of speeches celebrating the life of the deceased. Feasts of various sizes are held to mark the occasion, based on the economic or social circumstances of the deceased and his or her next of kin. Embalming practices also vary, ranging from simple to quite elaborate, based on the status of the deceased individual.

Ugandans celebrate a wide variety of other occasions, including birthdays, anniversaries, and graduation days. Festivals are also held to commemorate successful harvests, the arts, and literacy. While these festivals are often fairly simple in nature, Ugandans never miss an opportunity to celebrate personal or communal achievements with their family, friends, and neighbors.

INTERNET LINKS

https://www.newvision.co.ug/new_vision/news/1298949/sending-loved-ones-ugandan
This article from the Ugandan newspaper *New Vision* explores funeral practices among Uganda's many tribes, detailing many of the most unique beliefs and traditions still carried out in some parts of the country.

https://publicholidays.ug
All of Uganda's public holidays, religious and secular, are profiled here, with descriptions of the various holidays' origins and details about specific forms of celebration.

FOOD

Uganda's markets teem with fresh food, much of it transported great distances from private farms.

FOOD IS AN IMPORTANT PART OF Ugandan society. It is featured prominently in festivals and other gatherings, be they in the cities or the countryside, and is used to bring communities together. Though local recipes and traditional African foods remain the principal means of sustenance for most Ugandans, the arrival of other cultural influences—especially through the British—means that a wide assortment of international foods can be found in urban restaurants. Indian and Thai food are particularly popular among city-dwellers. Food is also a precious resource for poor Ugandans, who struggle to find enough to feed themselves and their families. About 12 percent of the population today lives in hunger, and that number is expected to rise in the future.

13

"A united family eats from the same plate."
—Baganda proverb

A BLOODY GOOD MEAL

The Bahima and the Karamojong tribes traditionally used defibrinated, or processed, cattle blood as a source of food. It was believed that some of the characteristics of the animal would pass into those who consumed the blood, making them stronger or more powerful. Meat from the cattle would only be eaten at ceremonial occasions, with milk and blood harvested from living animals in a sustainable fashion. This tradition is still practiced to some degree today.

THE UGANDAN DIET

The staple foods cooked in a traditional Ugandan kitchen usually include meat (mainly from cattle and goats), fish, millet, corn, sorghum, beans, and various fruits and vegetables. *Matoke* (MA-toh-keh), a type of green banana, forms the basis for several different recipes, and milk products, including cheese and curd, are also commonly consumed. Popular meals include *nyama chomo*, or roasted meat, a tribal food that can be found today in most restaurants and bars, and *luwombo* and *oluwombo*. *Luwombo* is a spicy stew steamed in banana leaves, and *oluwombo* adds rice, chicken, and tomatoes to the mix. Other local delicacies are more basic, and include fried cassava, roasted sweet potatoes, and steamed yams.

A vast array of tropical fruit is available in Uganda, thanks to the lush vegetation growing high in the mountains throughout the country. Markets are held in most villages every day. Local women gather there to make their selection from the range of fresh produce on display. It is a social event as much as a domestic necessity, as it provides an opportunity for interaction with neighbors.

Tomatoes, avocados, cassava, *matoke*, and potatoes form part of a healthy, balanced diet. Rural tribes living in the savannas of Uganda traditionally based their diet solely on meat. Today, however, improved transportation and communications systems mean that every market has access to a supply of fresh fruits and vegetables, provided one can afford them.

Matoke is Uganda's national food and one of the oldest dishes in the world. It is popular in many parts of Uganda and is grown in almost every homestead in Buganda. When the matoke fruit is ready, the leaves are cut off and kept for cooking, together with the plant fibers, which are used to tie the leaves together during cooking. The stalks are put in the saucepan, too, together with the leaves, to ease the steaming process. Matoke can be eaten with many sauces, stews, curries, and vegetables.

FOOD PREPARATION

Before the use of gas and electricity in Uganda, kitchens were often built separately from the main house. Cooking was done mostly on open fires using firewood, charcoal, or animal dung for fuel. The separate hut kept fumes and smoke away from the main home. This is still the case in villages today. In large towns and cities, however, kitchens are a part of the house and are equipped with paraffin, electric, or gas stoves.

Traditional cooking and eating utensils included huge bamboo storage baskets, winnowing trays, grinding stones, and mortars and pestles, There was also an assortment of pots, dishes, calabashes, and gourds of all shapes and sizes, both to eat from and to use as mixing bowls. Modern utensils are becoming more common, but many Ugandans still eat using their hands, taking the food from a communal pot and using small saucers as dishes.

Mortars and pestles are used to pound millet and other grains.

COOKING FOR COMPANY

In the less sophisticated Ugandan kitchens, food is often prepared in quantities sufficient to feed a large extended family or several smaller families within one community. The staples of potatoes, cassava, *matoke*, and beans form the basis of most meals and can be cooked well ahead of time and left simmering while the family is out working. There is little variety in the daily menu prepared in a Ugandan kitchen—breakfast, lunch, and dinner often closely resemble one another. The selection depends on what is available at the market, or what fish or meat the male family members have been able to catch that day. Since meat is expensive and hard to come by in some parts of the country, starchy foods like potatoes, cassava, and millet are used generously to stretch meals and make them as filling as possible. Meat is used sparingly, when it is available, to add flavor and texture.

Food is very important at social gatherings, and communal eating is held in high regard; this means that Ugandans will find any excuse to gather their family and friends for a feast. A relative or friend visiting after a long absence can expect celebrations with music and dancing, as well as a table laden with food. On such occasions, the food is rarely elaborate, but there is lots of it, and it is prepared with care. Other important occasions, such as christenings, holidays, birthdays, and anniversaries, also feature big, celebratory feasts for anyone who wants to come.

BEVERAGES

In addition to milk and water, which are now obtained quite easily in many villages, most tribes brewed some form of beer that they drank with their meals. The Baganda made an alcoholic beer from bananas called *mwenge bigere* (m-wen-GAY bee-GER-ay), and a nonalcoholic type called *omubisi* (om-oo-BEE-see). The Bakiga made an alcoholic beer from sorghum called *omuranba* (om-oo-RAN-ba), while the Bahutu called their sorghum-based beer *amarwa* (ah-MAR-wa). Different types of beer are still popular in Uganda today. Nonalcoholic carbonated drinks imported from the West are available, but more popular are the local, cheaper alternatives.

TRIBAL FOOD TABOOS

In the past, each tribe in Uganda had certain rituals that had to be observed concerning what food could be eaten, by whom, and when. For instance, among the Karamojong, the meat from cows and goats was eaten only if the animals had died naturally, not if they had been killed for food. Among the Bagwe, women were not allowed to eat lungfish, chicken, or eggs. In the Bunyoro tribe, certain foods were reserved for particular functions, such as guest meals, which always consisted of millet and meat. Potatoes were never given to guests, except in times of scarcity. Among the Iteso, the men did not eat with the women; instead, they ate separately, seated on stools, tree stumps, or stones, while the women sat on mats in a circle around the food. Among the Basamia, the Bagwe, and the Banyole, women and girls ate together from one plate, while boys and men ate together from another. Unnecessary talking was not allowed at mealtimes. While these customs have largely died out among urban Ugandans, many food taboos are still observed by the most traditional elements of the country's tribes.

Despite coffee being Uganda's number-one export and a way of life for a significant portion of the population, it is actually not very popular with most Ugandans. They prefer a milky, spiced tea. While some Ugandans are unable to afford the price of processed coffee, for most it is simply a matter of taste; coffee drinking just has not caught on in the country. Some enterprising Ugandans are attempting to change this by opening roasteries and cafés in Kampala and other large urban areas. These establishments provide employment opportunities and homegrown coffee, but their clientele remains mostly tourists.

FOOD INSECURITY

While most Ugandans consume an adequate amount of food and have regular access to either markets or their own farms, a portion of the population struggles to find enough to eat. About 12 percent of Ugandans are chronically food insecure, and nearly 25 percent are food stressed. Food insecurity refers to the inability to reliably access a sufficient quantity of affordable food, while food stress indicates hardships in acquiring food that do not totally prevent a person from eating regularly. For the millions of people dealing with these problems, that means that they do not consume enough calories in a day to properly sustain themselves, and their children have no food to eat at school (if they even attend). Ten and a half percent of children under the age of five are underweight, and more than 30 percent have experienced some degree of growth stunting. This problem is worse in rural areas, where the food insecurity crisis is more keenly felt. The food shortage is caused by a variety of factors. Changing rainfall patterns and extended droughts lead to lower crop yields, reducing the raw amount of food available. On top of that, with so much of the Ugandan economy based on agriculture, a poor yield will devastate some farmers' incomes, preventing them from having enough money to buy food from markets to supplement what they have grown for themselves. Small farmers also lack refined skills and knowledge of proper handling techniques, often storing their crops in improper conditions that lead to spoilage and

Children are particularly vulnerable to food insecurity in Uganda. Lack of proper nutrition can lead to growth stunting and serious health problems.

reducing the amount they have to sell. Since so many farmers are poor, they also have no access to credit or insurance to guard against a bad year.

The government and the United Nations' World Food Programme (WFP) have worked together to greater or lesser degrees since the country's independence in 1962. In recent years, the WFP has worked with the government to provide food and/or cash assistance to those affected by food shortages, as well as training to those willing to build farms, orchards, and irrigation systems. They have also taught farmers crop diversification techniques to guard against the failure of one particular crop, as well as other practices to protect quality and increase productivity. Though this may prove to be an effective short-term solution for some Ugandans, the scale of the problem will only increase. Massive droughts in the Horn of Africa over the last decade have exposed tens of millions of people to famine across the region, and climate change is likely to produce more (and more extreme) cases in the future. Uganda, and East Africa as a whole, needs internationally funded, long-term solutions to prevent a humanitarian catastrophe of vast proportions.

INTERNET LINKS

http://www.ugandatourist.com/food-dining/uganda-recipes
The food culture of Uganda is profiled here, with discussions of regional specialties and tribal customs relating to food.

http://www1.wfp.org/countries/uganda
The World Food Programme's profile of Uganda contains information about the extent of the crisis posed by food insecurity in the country, as well as details about programs the WFP is launching to help alleviate the hunger faced by so many Ugandans.

MATOKE

Ugandan Beef and Plantain Stew

6—8 plantains or *matokes*, peeled and diced
1 lemon, juice only
2—3 tablespoons oil
1 onion, chopped
1 green pepper, chopped
3—4 cloves garlic, minced
1—2 green chili peppers, finely chopped
 (optional)
¾ tablespoon ground coriander, or to taste
1 pound stewing beef, cubed (optional)
2 cups tomatoes, seeded and chopped
2 cups water or beef stock
Salt, to taste

Peel the plantains, cut into cubes, sprinkle with lemon juice, and set aside.

Heat the oil in a large pot or pan over a medium-high flame. Add the onions and green pepper, and sauté until the onion is cooked through and translucent, about 3 or 4 minutes. Add the garlic, chili peppers, and coriander, and sauté for another minute or so.

Stir in the beef (if using) and tomatoes and cook for another 2 or 3 minutes.

Add the beef stock or water and season with salt. Bring to a boil, then reduce heat to medium-low heat, cover, and simmer for about 20 minutes.

Stir in the plantains, cover, and simmer for another 30 to 40 minutes, or until the beef is tender and the plantains have softened. Adjust seasoning and serve hot.

LUWOMBO

2 pounds beef, diced

1 cup unsalted peanuts, ground

2 onions, chopped

4 tomatoes, chopped, or 1 (14 oz.) can of crushed tomatoes

1 cube chicken bouillon

1 cup mushrooms, sliced

1 piece smoked fish, or smoked meat (optional)

Oil for cooking

Salt

Pepper

Banana leaves

6 plantains

Before making, ask an adult for help.

Sauté the meat in a lightly oiled pan until browned on all sides. Set aside.

Heat a tablespoon of oil in a pan, then add the onions and cook for 2 minutes before adding the tomatoes, chicken bouillon cube, salt, pepper, peanuts, mushrooms, and smoked fish (or smoked meat). If necessary, add a little water to form a smooth sauce. Simmer for 8 to 10 minutes.

Add meat and mix.

Cut banana leaves to form 10-inch-wide rectangles. Remove the mid rib.

Place the banana leaves above a fire for a few seconds to soften. Then rinse with water.

Place a portion of the meat mixture in the center of a leaf.

Fold the leaf on the sides, then fold the other two ends to form a small pouch.

Tie with a string, then repeat the operation with the rest of the mixture.

Place a rack in the bottom of a large pot and add water to the bottom. Place the pouches on top of the rack and cover.

Add the plantains over the pouches in the pan. Bring to a boil and steam for at least two hours.

Take plantains out of the pot and mash with a fork.

Serve *luwombo* with mashed plantains

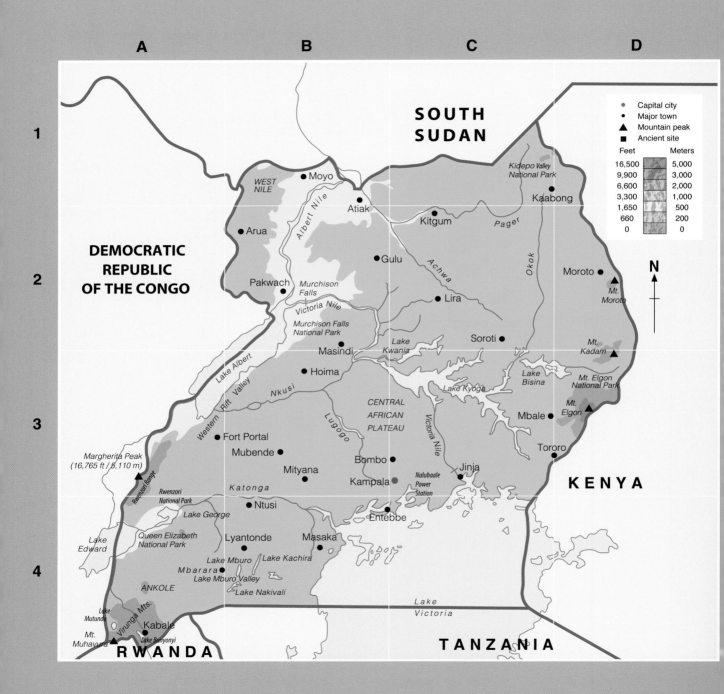

MAP OF UGANDA

Achwa River, C2
Albert Nile, B1—B2
Ankole, A4
Arua, B2
Atiak, B1

Bombo, C3

Central African Plateau, B3, C3

Democratic Republic of the Congo, A1—A4, B1—B2

Entebbe, B4

Fort Portal, A3

Gulu, B2

Hoima, B3

Jinja, C3

Kaabong, C1
Kabale, A4
Kampala, C3
Katonga, B3
Kenya, D1—D4

Kidepo Valley National Park, C1
Kitgum, C2

Lake Albert, A3, B2—B3
Lake Bisina, C3, D3
Lake Bunyonyi, A4
Lake Edward, A4
Lake George, A4
Lake Kachira, B4
Lake Kwania, C2—C3
Lake Kyoga, C3
Lake Mburo, B4
Lake Mburo Valley, A4, B4
Lake Mutunda, A4
Lake Nakivali, B4
Lake Victoria, B4, C3—C4, D4
Lira, C2
Lugogo River, B3
Lyantonde, B4

Margherita Peak, A3
Masaka, B4
Masindi, B2
Mbale, C3
Mbarara, A4
Mityana, B3

Moroto, D2
Moyo, B1
Mount Elgon, D3
Mount Elgon National Park, D3
Mount Kadam, D3
Mount Moroto, D2
Mount Muhavura, A4
Mubende, B3
Murchison Falls, B2
Murchinson Falls National Park, B2

Nalubaale Power Station, C3
Nkusi River, A3, B3
Ntusi, B4

Okok River, C1—C2

Pager River, C1, D1
Pakwach, B2

Queen Elizabeth National Park, A4

Rwanda, A4

Rwenzori Mountains National, A3—A4
Rwenzori Range, A3—A4

Soroti, C2
South Sudan, A1, B1, C1, D1

Tanzania, A4, B4, C4, D4
Tororo, C3, D3

Victoria Nile, C3
Virunga Mountains, A4

West Nile, B1
Western Rift Valley, A3, B3

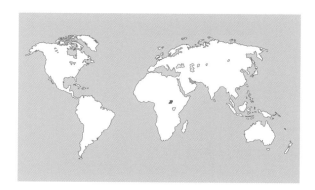

ECONOMIC UGANDA

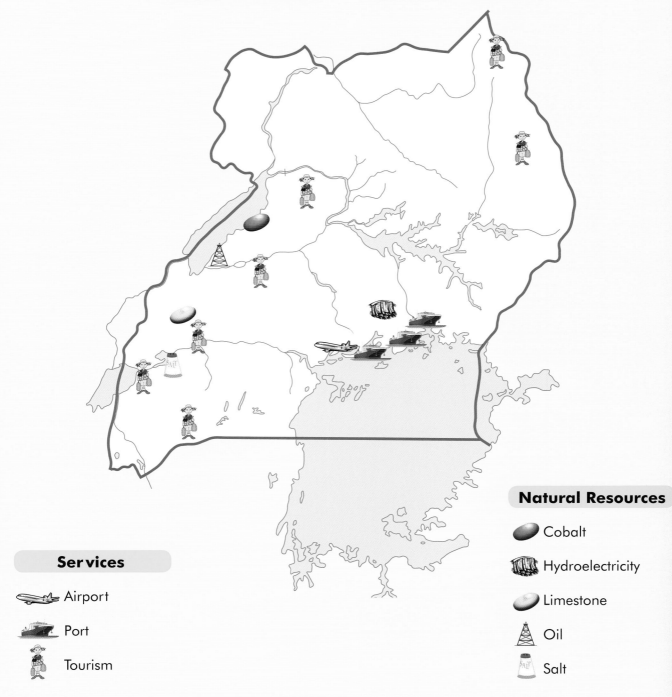

Services

✈ Airport

🚢 Port

🧳 Tourism

Natural Resources

Cobalt

Hydroelectricity

Limestone

Oil

Salt

ABOUT THE ECONOMY

OVERVIEW

The economy of Uganda is heavily dependent on agriculture, which employs over 70 percent of the country's workforce. Coffee is the number-one export in Uganda, accounting for 16 percent of all exports. The country also possesses sizable mineral deposits of gold, copper, and cobalt. The economy has been stabilized by President Yoweri Museveni following an economic collapse and a civil war, and experienced steady growth throughout the 1990s and 2000s. Growth plateaued in the early 2010s, however, as the global recession reduced the amount of foreign capital coming into the country, and climate change reduced crop yields. Uganda is counting on renewed foreign investment and revenues generated from its oil reserves to spur further growth in the future, and to begin offsetting the country's growing debts.

GROSS DOMESTIC PRODUCT (GDP)

$26.62 billion (2017 estimate)

GDP GROWTH

4.8 percent (2017 estimate)

CURRENCY

Shilling
$1 = 3,760 shillings (October 2018)

LAND USE

Arable land, 34.3 percent; permanent crops, 11.3 percent; permanent pasture, 25.6 percent; forest, 14.5 percent; other, 14.3 percent

NATURAL RESOURCES

Copper, cobalt, hydropower, limestone, salt, arable land, gold, oil

AGRICULTURAL PRODUCTS

Coffee, tea, cotton, tobacco, cassava, potatoes, corn, millet, pulses, cut flowers, beef, goat meat, milk, poultry, fish

MAJOR EXPORTS

Coffee, fish and fish products, tea, cotton, flowers, horticultural products, gold

MAJOR IMPORTS

Capital equipment, vehicles, petroleum, medical supplies, cereals

MAIN TRADE PARTNERS

Kenya, China, India, United Arab Emirates, Democratic Republic of the Congo, Japan, Saudi Arabia, Rwanda

WORK FORCE

15.84 million

UNEMPLOYMENT RATE

9.4 percent

INFLATION

5.6 percent (2017 estimate)

EXTERNAL DEBT

$10.8 billion (2018 estimate)

CULTURAL UGANDA

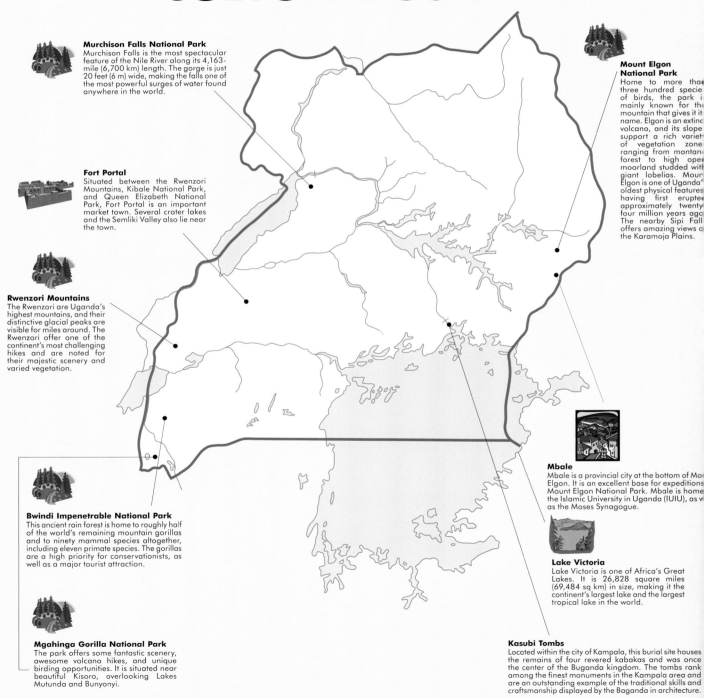

Murchison Falls National Park
Murchison Falls is the most spectacular feature of the Nile River along its 4,163-mile (6,700 km) length. The gorge is just 20 feet (6 m) wide, making the falls one of the most powerful surges of water found anywhere in the world.

Fort Portal
Situated between the Rwenzori Mountains, Kibale National Park, and Queen Elizabeth National Park, Fort Portal is an important market town. Several crater lakes and the Semliki Valley also lie near the town.

Rwenzori Mountains
The Rwenzori are Uganda's highest mountains, and their distinctive glacial peaks are visible for miles around. The Rwenzori offer one of the continent's most challenging hikes and are noted for their majestic scenery and varied vegetation.

Bwindi Impenetrable National Park
This ancient rain forest is home to roughly half of the world's remaining mountain gorillas and to ninety mammal species altogether, including eleven primate species. The gorillas are a high priority for conservationists, as well as a major tourist attraction.

Mgahinga Gorilla National Park
The park offers some fantastic scenery, awesome volcano hikes, and unique birding opportunities. It is situated near beautiful Kisoro, overlooking Lakes Mutunda and Bunyonyi.

Mount Elgon National Park
Home to more than three hundred species of birds, the park is mainly known for the mountain that gives it its name. Elgon is an extinct volcano, and its slopes support a rich variety of vegetation zones ranging from montane forest to high open moorland studded with giant lobelias. Mount Elgon is one of Uganda's oldest physical features, having first erupted approximately twenty-four million years ago. The nearby Sipi Falls offers amazing views of the Karamoja Plains.

Mbale
Mbale is a provincial city at the bottom of Mount Elgon. It is an excellent base for expeditions to Mount Elgon National Park. Mbale is home to the Islamic University in Uganda (IUIU), as well as the Moses Synagogue.

Lake Victoria
Lake Victoria is one of Africa's Great Lakes. It is 26,828 square miles (69,484 sq km) in size, making it the continent's largest lake and the largest tropical lake in the world.

Kasubi Tombs
Located within the city of Kampala, this burial site houses the remains of four revered kabakas and was once the center of the Buganda kingdom. The tombs rank among the finest monuments in the Kampala area and are an outstanding example of the traditional skills and craftsmanship displayed by the Baganda in architecture.

ABOUT THE CULTURE

OFFICIAL NAME
Republic of Uganda

FLAG DESCRIPTION
Black, yellow, and red stripes repeated horizontally, with the national emblem, the crested crane, in the middle

TOTAL AREA
93,065 square miles (241,038 sq km)

CAPITAL
Kampala

ETHNIC GROUPS
Baganda, 16.5 percent; Banyankole, 9.6 percent; Basoga, 8.8 percent; Bakiga, 7.1 percent; Iteso, 7.0 percent; Langi, 6.3 percent; Bagisu, 4.9 percent; Acholi, 4.4 percent; Lugbara, 3.3 percent; others, 32.1 percent

RELIGION
Christianity, 84.4 percent (Roman Catholic, 39.3 percent; Anglican, 32.0 percent; Pentecostal, 11.1 percent; Seventh-Day Adventist, 1.7 percent);

Muslim, 13.7 percent; others, 1.6 percent; none, 0.2 percent

BIRTH RATE
42.4 births per 1,000 Ugandans (2018 estimate)

DEATH RATE
9.9 deaths per 1,000 Ugandans (2018 estimate)

AGE STRUCTURE
0—14 years, 48 percent; 15—64 years, 50 percent; 65 years and over, 2 percent (2017 estimate)

MAIN LANGUAGES
English and Swahili (official national languages), Luganda (most widely used of the Niger-Congo languages), other Niger-Congo languages, Nilo-Saharan languages, Arabic

LITERACY
People aged 15 and above who can both read and write: 78.4 percent

RECENT POLITICAL LEADERS
Milton Obote, president, 1966—1971, 1980—1985
Idi Amin, president, 1971—1979
Yusuf Kironde Lule, president, 1979
Godfrey Lukongwa Binaisa, president, 1979—1980
Paulo Muwanga, president, 1980
Tito Okello, president, 1985—1986
Yoweri Kaguta Museveni, president, 1986—present

TIMELINE

IN UGANDA	IN THE WORLD
	116–117 CE The Roman Empire reaches its greatest extent under Emperor Trajan (in power 98–117).
	1206–1368 Genghis Khan unifies the Mongols and starts conquest of the world.
	1530 Beginning of transatlantic slave trade organized by the Portuguese in Africa.
circa 1600 CE Bito dynasties of Buganda, Bunyoro, and Ankole founded.	
	1789–1799 The French Revolution.
1860s European explorers and missionaries enter Uganda.	
1894 Uganda becomes a British protectorate.	**1884–1885** The Berlin Conference divides the continent of Africa between the various European powers.
1900 Buganda Agreement formalizes the roles of the British and the Buganda kingdom.	
	1939–1945 World War II.
	1945–1991 Cold War between the United States and the Soviet Union.
1962 Uganda becomes independent.	
1966 Milton Obote drives Kabaka Mutesa II from the country and abolishes the tribal kingdoms.	**1966** The Chinese Cultural Revolution.
1971 Obote is toppled in coup led by Idi Amin.	
1972 Amin expels Uganda's Asian population.	
1976 Idi Amin declares himself president for life.	**1975** The fall of Saigon marks the end of the Vietnam War.
1978–1979 Amin launches invasion of Tanzania; counter-invasion succeeds in removing him from power.	

IN UGANDA	IN THE WORLD
1980	
Milton Obote elected president; National Resistance Movement (NRM) launches to oppose his rule.	
1985	
Obote is deposed in military coup.	
1986	**1986**
National Resistance Army rebels take Kampala and install Yoweri Museveni as president.	The space shuttle *Challenger* explodes.
Late 1980s	
The Lord's Resistance Army (LRA) begins carrying out terrorist activities in northern Uganda.	**1991** Breakup of the Soviet Union.
1995	
A new constitution is promulgated; Museveni is formally elected president early the next year.	**1997** Hong Kong is returned to China.
2001	**2001**
East African Community (EAC) inaugurated.	Terrorists crash planes into New York, Washington, DC, and Pennsylvania.
	2003 United States launches invasion of Iraq.
	2004
2005	Eleven Asian countries hit by a giant tsunami, killing at least 225,000 people.
A referendum opens Ugandan politics to multiple parties; presidential term limits are abolished.	
2006	
President Museveni wins multiparty elections.	
2008	
Ugandan, Southern Sudanese, and DRC armies launch offensive against LRA bases.	
2011	**2011–2013**
Museveni wins another disputed election.	A severe drought causes mass famine across East Africa.
	2013–2016 Ebola virus epidemic in West Africa.
2016	**2016–2017**
Museveni wins reelection.	Another severe drought strikes East Africa.
2017	
Age limit for presidential candidates lifted; Robert Kyagulanyi (Bobi Wine) elected to Parliament.	

GLOSSARY

abalokole (ah-ba-LO-KO-li)
Christian converts.

baami (BAA-mee)
Baganda chiefs.

bakopi (BA-koh-pee)
Serfs in Baganda society.

balangira (BA-lan-gee-ra)
Baganda princes.

defibrinate
To process blood by removing fibrin from it.

homestead
Self-sufficient rural home with a plot of land to keep animals and grow crops.

imperialism
The extension of a state's power through the formal or informal acquisition of political and economic control over other territories.

indaro (in-DA-ro)
Religious shrine of the Basamia and the Bagwe.

kabaka (ka-BA-ka)
Tribal king of the Baganda.

kanzu (KAN-zoo)
Traditional Baganda attire.

matoke (MA-toh-keh)
A type of green banana.

mbaga (m-BAG-ah)
Dance honoring occasions such as weddings and royal gatherings.

mirembe (mee-REM-bay)
Peace.

misambwa (mi-SAM-bwa)
Spirits of the dead living in the form of natural objects, such as trees or stones.

mizimu (mi-ZEE-moo)
Ghost of the dead believed by the Baganda to haunt living enemies of the dead person.

nalinya (NA-leen-ya)
Royal sister in Baganda society.

namasole (NA-ma-so-lay)
Queen mother in Baganda society.

okwabya olumbe (ok-wa-by-YA o-LOOM-bay)
Funeral rites.

okwalula abaana (ok-wa-loo-LA ah-BA-na)
Ceremony in which children are given clan names.

okwanjula (ok-wan-JOO-la)
Formal introduction of the prospective husband and his family to the bride-to-be and her family before an arranged marriage.

protectorate
A territory that retains some level of internal autonomy while remaining under the overall control of a more powerful state.

FOR FURTHER INFORMATION

BOOKS

Akallo, Grace, and Faith J. H. McDonnell. *Girl Soldier: A Story of Hope for Northern Uganda's Children*. Ada, MI: Chosen Books, 2007.

Blauer, Ettagale, and Jason Laure. *Uganda*. Enchantment of the World. New York: Scholastic Library Publishing, revised edition, 2009.

Braun, Eric. *Uganda in Pictures*. Visual Geography. Minneapolis: Lerner Publications, 2005.

Briggs, Philip. *Uganda*. Buckinghamshire, UK: Bradt Travel Guides, eighth edition, 2017.

Hattersley, Charles W. *Uganda by Pen and Camera*. BiblioBazaar, 2008.

Kubuitsile, Lauri. *Uganda*. The Evolution of Africa's Major Nations. Philadelphia: Mason Crest Publishers, 2013.

Otiso, Kefa M. *Culture and Customs of Uganda*. Culture and Customs of Africa. Westport, CT: Greenwood Press, 2006.

Reid, Richard J. *A History of Modern Uganda*. Cambridge, UK: Cambridge University Press, 2017.

Rice, Andrew. *The Teeth May Smile but the Heart Does Not Forget: Murder and Memory in Uganda*. London, UK: Picador, 2010.

Sweikar, Michael. *Mzungu: A Notre Dame Student in Uganda*. Nashville: Cold Tree Press, 2007.

Tucker, Alfred R. *Eighteen Years in Uganda and East Africa*. BiblioBazaar, 2009.

MUSIC

Benon and Vamposs. *I Know*. CreateSpace, 2008.

Magoola, Rachel. *Songs from the Source of the Nile*. Arc Music, October 2007.

Okello, Omega Bugembe. *Kiwomera Emmeeme*. Comin Atcha Distribution Group, 2008.

Wine, Bobi. *Kyarenga*. Fire Base, 2018.

MOVIES

God Loves Uganda. Variance Films, 2013.

The Last King of Scotland. 20th Century Fox, 2007.

Queen of Katwe. Walt Disney Pictures, 2016.

BIBLIOGRAPHY

Central Intelligence Agency. *The World Factbook, Uganda*. 2018 update. https://www.cia.gov/library/publications/the-world-factbook/geos/ug.html.

Coughlan, Sean. "Tackling Uganda's Lack of School Places." BBC News, January 8, 2014. https://www.bbc.com/news/business-25304848.

Finnström, Sverker. *Living with Bad Surroundings: War, History, and Everyday Moments in Northern Uganda*. The Cultures and Practice of Violence. Durham, NC: Duke University Press, 2008.

Fitzpatrick, Mary. *Lonely Planet East Africa*. Victoria, Australia: Lonely Planet, 8th edition, 2009.

Hanson, Thor. *The Impenetrable Forest: My Gorilla Years in Uganda*. New York: Curtis Brown Unlimited, revised edition, 2008.

Kisa, Emma Laura N. "Women in Uganda More Likely to Experience Domestic Violence Than Men." *Daily Monitor*, March 8, 2018. http://www.monitor.co.ug/OpEd/Commentary/Women-Uganda-domestic-violence-men-assault-/689364-4333592-18v7cr/index.html.

Leggett, Ian. *Uganda*. Oxfam Country Profiles Series. Oxford, UK: Oxfam Publishing, 2001.

Musinguzi, Bamuturaki. "The Trouble with Art in Uganda." *East African*, May 16, 2011. http://www.theeastafrican.co.ke/magazine/The-trouble-with-art-in-Uganda/434746-1162826-ege6u5/index.html.

Musisi, Frederic. "China Seeks to Further Ties with Uganda." *Daily Monitor*, June 16, 2018. http://www.monitor.co.ug/News/National/China-seeks-further-ties-Uganda/688334-4614846-6fdq43/index.html.

Sweikar, Michael. *Mzungu: A Notre Dame Student in Uganda*. Nashville, TN: Cold Tree Press, 2007.

"Uganda Country Profile." BBC News, May 10, 2018. https://www.bbc.co.uk/news/world-africa-14107906.

United Nations Development Programme. *Human Development Reports, Uganda*. 2016. http://hdr.undp.org/en/countries/profiles/UGA.

US Department of Commerce. *Uganda Country Commercial Guide: Labor Policies and Practices*. August 3, 2017. https://www.export.gov/article?id=Uganda-Labor-Policies-and-Practices.

US Department of State. *Uganda*. Country Reports on Human Rights Practices for 2017. https://www.state.gov/j/drl/rls/hrrpt/humanrightsreport/index.htm#wrapper.

"Water, Sanitation, and Hygiene (WASH)." Uganda Village Project. Accessed September 14, 2018. http://www.ugandavillageproject.org/what-we-do/healthy-villages/hygiene-sanitation.

INDEX

INDEX